THE APPRENTICE WRITER

JULIAN GREEN

THE APPRENTICE WRITER

Marion Boyars
New York · London

First published in the United States and Great Britain in 1993
by Marion Boyars Publishers
237 East 39th Street New York NY 10016
24 Lacy Road London SW15 1NL

Distributed in Australia by
Peribo Pty Ltd, Terrey Hills, NSW

© Julian Green, 1987 (*Le langage et son double*)
© Editions du Seuil, 1991 (*L'homme et son ombre*)

English texts extracted from *L'homme et son ombre*, originally published by Editions
du Seuil, Paris, in 1991 and *Le langage et son double* published by Editions du Seuil,
Paris, in 1987

Library of Congress Cataloging-in-Publication Data

Green, Julian, 1900–
      The apprentice writer / Julian Green.
      1.   Green, Julian, 1900–   —Biography.   2. Green, Julian, 1900–
—Authorship.   3. Authors, French—20th century—Biography.
4. Authors, American—20th century—Biography.   5. France–
–Intellectual life—20th century.   6. Fiction—Technique.
      I. Title.
PQ2613.R3Z462   1992
843'.912—dc20   92–22818
[B]

British Library Cataloguing in Publication Data

Green, Julian
The Apprentice Writer
      I. Title
      844.912

      ISBN 0-7145-2956-7 Cloth

Typeset by Regent Typesetting, London
Printed and bound in Great Britain by
Biddles Ltd, Guildford and King's Lynn

Contents

About the Author

Born in 1900 of American parents living in Paris, Julian Green has spent most of his extraordinary literary career there, writing now in French for a wide and enthusiastic readership. He has published over sixty books in France: novels, essays, plays, a four-volume autobiography and, so far, fourteen volumes of his journals. Initially writing in English – and this volume collects for the first time his writings in that language – he published a number of celebrated books in England and the United States before writing almost exclusively in French.

As an American, Julian Green is the only foreign member of the Académie Française. He is also a member of the American Academy of Arts and Letters, winner of the Harper Prize, the Prix Marcel Proust, the Prix France-Amérique, the Prix Cavour and numerous other international awards. He is also one of the few living authors to have their collected works published in the prestigious Gallimard Pléiade series.

Julian Green's epic novel of the antebellum South, *The Distant Lands*, was published in 1991 simultaneously with his play, *South*, which is set on the eve of the Civil War. His book of essays about Paris with a selection of the author's own photographs of his favorite city is available from the same publishers who are also publishing his autobiography in four volumes. The sequel to *The Distant Lands*, set during the Civil War, will be published in 1993.

Julian Green lives in Paris.

An American in Paris

Julian Green's life is a series of paradoxes: American from the South, but born in Paris. A quarter Welsh, a quarter Scots, a quarter Irish, a quarter English = one American, he says himself. Born in Paris, he spoke only English with his mother; 'We never exchanged a single word in any other language. With an outburst of tenderness she would clasp me to her and call me "my little French boy ..."'

As a young student at the University of Virginia, it was in English that he began to write. His first story, *The Apprentice Psychiatrist*, so captivated his Professor of Literature and his fellow undergraduates that it got published immediately in May 1920 — the author was 19 — in the very exclusive Virginia Quarterly Review. *English* writer ...

But back in Paris, after he had completed his studies, Julian Green took to writing in the language of his native land and from his first books became one of the French literary personalities of the century; one of the very rare living authors to see his work included in the prestigious Bibliotèque de la Pleïade, with 6 volumes already published. *French* writer ...

However, he didn't stop making numerous trips to the United States and to England where he received the Bookman Prize in 1929 in London for *Leviathan* at the same time as Virginia Woolf was honored for *To the Lighthouse*. He was also awarded many prizes in the United States to which he returned quite naturally as an American when the Nazis invaded Europe.

He then took up his mother tongue again, published his memoirs, wrote articles and short stories, but at the same time was called up to Camp Ritchie and was then reassigned to the Office of War Information (OWI) and put in charge of the Voice of America for whom he broadcast every day to France.

When his book *Memories of Happy Days* appeared in 1942, John Calvin Metcalfe, the same professor at the University of Virginia who had been responsible for publishing his first piece, wrote to him: 'One would think it your native tongue, as it is your ancestral. And I am sure you have inherited it, enriched by your wide reading, from your Southern parents, especially from your dear Mother ... I take great personal pride in your lucid idiomatic style. I remember you once said to me, when you were a student here, that you wrote in French much better than you did in English. Well, if you still do — but I don't believe it!'

The pieces collected in this volume form a part of Julian Green's English output, written and published between 1919 and 1944. 'In English I am someone other,' he has said. 'My dreams are mostly in English, and it was in English that I learned The Lord's Prayer from my mother. It's in English that my emotions flow most naturally, as well as words of affection or love.'

The theme of the double is, moreover, one of the major themes in his works. So far from what one would believe, it does not refer to a writer changing his language, but to a different writer, *another*, as if he had two personalities.

Giovanni Lucera
Translated by Arthur Boyars

Memories of Happy Days

These three fragments were written in 1940. Julian
Green had originally intended to write his auto-
biography in English (he later wrote all four volumes
in French) while he was in America during the
Second World War. Instead he wrote a book called
Memories of Happy Days which was published by
Harper in the United States and by Dent in Great
Britain in 1942 and won the Book of the Month
prize. The material in this essay is expanded upon in
the first two volumes of Green's autobiography, *The
Green Paradise* and *The War at Sixteen*, published in an
English translation by Marion Boyars Publishers.

The coming of tango

Just about this time, the tango came into fashion and somehow it seemed to dispel any sad thoughts brought on by the slaughter in distant Serbia. I knew from certain hushed whispers and horrified raising of eyebrows that the tango was supposed to be a naughty dance. Decent people frowned on it and old Pope Pius the Tenth was so pained by its growing success that he tried to have another dance introduced to take its place, the prim Venetian Furlana, which one danced at a distance of two or three feet from one's partner, preferably with a *fazzoletto* or handkerchief in one's hand. Parisians looked on and grinned, their faith in tango unperturbed.

In those days, my sister Retta took piano lessons from a black-eyed lady by the name of Mme de Las Palmas. As I remember her, this lady wore a slight moustache and smelt faintly like a zoo, but her rendering of Sinding's *Frühling*[1] was, to a certain extent, a sort of compensation. Anyhow she taught my sister to play Clementi correctly and to this day I can listen to that gentleman's simple tunes with pleasure, because they bring up so many memories of happy days.

It is a terrible leap from Clementi to tango, but Retta was unafraid. One afternoon she came home with an album which she had purchased with her monthly allowance. On the cover was a picture of a gaucho with full lips and half-closed eyes dancing with an equally exotic looking lady. My sister went to the piano, opened her album with a firm hand and began to play. Her face wore a frown and the tip of her tongue stuck out between her teeth. I don't think she could have been more than fifteen, as her hair was still down her back, and she played as only a young girl can play who has studied Clementi; there was nothing languorous about her touch, it was bold and firm, and as straightforward as she was herself; in fact, I have never known anyone who missed the point of tango with such utter innocence, but she was determined to learn this music, and learn it she did.

My mother, who had no ear at all and could hardly tell a hymn from the Star Spangled Banner, was probably unaware of her daughter's doings and would have cared very little had she known that *Dans tes bras* was being performed on our piano instead of the *Sonatine pour délier les doigts*. She was far too kind and liberal-minded to suspect evil where no evil was, and so Retta was allowed to forge ahead unhampered and unvexed. There came a day when she finally mastered two or three South American pieces and I can still see her intent expression as she played, her vigorous little hands patiently striking the keyboard, making the brass candlesticks quiver and jingle. I don't know what Mme de Las Palmas thought of this. Doubtless she was not informed.

By 1913, everyone was dancing the tango in some form or other. Mothers looked on as their daughters were instructed at Baraduc's dancing school where Mr. Washington Lopp gave a *comme il faut* version of the new step.

War at sixteen

War experiences are as a rule so dull that I cannot bring myself to dwell on mine at great length, although I feel that they have enriched me in many ways. I shall therefore be as brief as I can.

Summer drew to a close and still we had not seen any action. After dark, when everything was quiet, I used to go to the foot of the garden and stand on a terrace overlooking a valley. Then, through the stillness of the night, a low, rumbling sound reached my ears, the distant thunder of Verdun. It never seemed to stop or diminish in intensity; one could hear it every night; it was impossible to imagine that it could go on forever and yet I could not see why it should ever relent. I listened to it with a beating heart and watched the sinister glimmering just above the horizon. This spoke far more than anything I had ever read or heard about the war, and I felt that the years to come could never obliterate this moment from my memory.

By October, they began sending us to certain points of the Argonne forest[2] where it was thought that our help might be needed, although that sector was quiet enough for the moment. On alternate nights, two ambulances were dispatched, each one carrying two men. I was very eager to go and finally my turn came; but as Mr. Ware[3] was still a little suspicious of my driving, I was not allowed to do more than sit by the driver. The latter, whom I shall call Johnson, was a theological student, a Unitarian, and spoke very little except when the subject of religion was mentioned, whereupon his bony face would glow and his steel rimmed spectacles glitter as if, in some unaccountable way, they shared his metaphysical raptures. He and I rarely exchanged views, but we were friendly.

We left Clermont and, having driven for a mile or two, reached the road which led to the forest of Argonne. It was a pitch black night and we were, of course, not allowed to use any other kind of light than a torch. Now our difficulties began. The road had been badly shelled and was riddled with holes, some of them large enough to contain a man. Indeed we soon found out that the enemy had not yet lost interest in this road, for a shell whined occasionally above our heads and exploded in the fields on our right. In spite of this we could not move very fast, although our instinct prompted us both to open the throttle as wide as we could in order to reach a safer spot.

'You had better get out and direct me,' said Johnson. 'When you come to a hole, whistle and I'll stop.'

I obeyed. Whenever I came to a shell-hole, I blew my whistle with all my might and felt tremendously important. Not once did it enter my mind that we could be hit by a shell. So on we crept for half an hour or so, circumventing shell-holes until we reached the forest where, for some reason, we felt quite safe, as if the trees were protecting us.

That night, we slept in a dug-out. Our beds were hardly raised above the ground; very primitive beds they were, made of a few boards hastily nailed together and a straw mattress. There was a table and a chair in one corner, an army blanket over the door to keep out the draughts, and on the ground, between two beds, a lantern which we were advised not to blow out; I soon understood why.

It was early and we talked a little before turning in. Once in a while we heard the strange hollow whistle of shells above the trees, but apart from that, the air was absolutely still. It seemed extraordinary to me to be in a dug-out with Johnson, and I am sure he felt the same way. I don't think he liked the place very much; all of a sudden he began talking about his home. He took off his glasses and wiped them. It was strange, his talking this way. Then he said something about religion and I grew more interested. He spoke of the enormous power which lies hidden in the Gospel and how the world would be affected by it in future times. The next thing he said took my breath away: he did not believe that there ever had been such a person as Christ, and it did not matter one way or the other, so long as we had the Gospels. What I answered, I do not remember, but I do know that I went to bed feeling extremely puzzled.

We did not undress, so as to be ready to leave immediately if a call came for us. Hardly had we lain down and ceased to talk when the reason for keeping the lantern burning made itself clear. Two or three very large rats began running about in the dark corners of the dug-out. Although at first they kept clear of the light, they soon became accustomed to it and all but upset it in their scurrying. I watched them for a minute and fell asleep.

I do not think more than an hour could have elapsed when a

French soldier came and woke us up, saying that there had been a call from a hospital in the neighborhood to transfer a wounded man to a more important sanitary base. So we jumped out of bed and left the dug-out, rubbing our eyes as we went. Quite a few shells whistled over our heads, and each time we fell flat on our stomachs as we had been told to do. Presently we came to the clearing where we had left our car, but the car wasn't there.

Thinking we had made a mistake in the location, we began walking through the woods, occasionally turning on the small flashlights which we were allowed to use, and it was not very long before I spied a strange object at my feet: it was a large fragment of wood painted gray, with a number which I instantly recognized as that of my ambulance. Now we looked in earnest and soon found scattered fragments of the lost Ford which a shell had apparently struck square in the middle and sent flying all over the woods. A great number of fragments were found later in the trees. There was nothing to do but to take the other car (two being sent out daily, as I have explained) and drive to the hospital, which we did.

By the end of the month, all of us having had a taste of war, we were sent to places a little nearer the front lines. The most uncomfortable of these places was a little village called Neuvilly. To be precise, nothing remained of this village except its name which was written on a sign-post near the spot where the Mairie had stood. Several times a day, in a perfunctory sort of way, this desolate spot was shelled, it being known to the Germans that first aid to the wounded was given there in a shelter. Early in October, my turn came to go to Neuvilly. I had been given numerous instructions by Mr. Ware, and during the time of respite drove to the shelter with a thrill of excitement.

I was greeted by a French officer whose name was, let us say, Jalin. Lieutenant Jalin was one of the strangest characters I have ever met. He was about thirty and seemed overjoyed at finding out that I spoke French as well as he did, because, he

said, my American comrades were incomprehensible and he
was dying of boredom from lack of conversation.

'I am very sorry I can't put you up comfortably,' he said as
we stepped down into a cellar. 'You will have to sleep on one of
your own stretchers, over there,' (he pointed to a dark corner)
'but,' he added with a gracious smile, 'I can provide you with a
pair of sheets. There is nothing like sleeping between sheets.'

I agreed.

Having showed me my bedroom, he took me to what he
called his dining-room, which was also in a cellar, but a well-
lighted cellar, with a round table, several chairs and a number
of books neatly placed on top of a trunk.

'There is a little barn at the back of our place,' he said after a
few minutes' conversation. 'Park your car there, but drive in
carefully.'

I obeyed. What he called a barn was really little else than a
shed, and I instantly understood why I had been told to drive in
carefully, when I saw a dead soldier lying on a stretcher. He
had been covered up with a blanket.

I parked my car and went back to the shelter where my host
offered me a cup of coffee.

Of course, I did not mention what I had seen in the shed,
although my mind reverted to it now and then with mixed
feelings of horror and sadness. I remember that we talked about
books. Lieutenant Jalin was very fond of literature, particularly
poetry. He knew a lot of poetry by heart and regaled me with
some of Albert Samain's voluptuous, if mediocre, lines; these he
recited with a quick, detached tone of voice and an occasional
outburst of enthusiasm which sent the blood to my cheeks. He
had a hard, white face with very black hair, and wore the
ribbon of the *médaille militaire* (the highest military award in
France) on his shabby uniform.

'You had better stay in the shelter,' he said, when I spoke of
going out. 'We are only a mile from the front lines. It is safer
here.'

On and on we talked of Anatole France and Pierre Louÿs and Claude Farrère until dinner-time, whereupon the lieutenant's orderly appeared to set the table which, to my surprise, he covered with a tablecloth of the finest texture. It had been quite a long time since I had seen a tablecloth and I could not help looking at this one with a certain degree of admiration; this seemed to flatter my host.

'As you perceive, I am well cared for here by the army administration,' he said with a smile. 'They send me more winding-sheets than we would possibly need and I keep a few for my own private use. Besides,' he added under his breath, 'what do the poor fellows care about being wrapped up in a sheet when they are dead?'

This sounded sensible enough, in a gruesome sort of way, and I ate my meal as heartily as I could. We talked for a while after dinner and I retired to my cellar and got into bed. The lieutenant's orderly had made up my bed for me, very neatly, I must say, but although I had looked forward to this moment, some two or three hours before, I now felt differently and knew too much about my sheets to relish the thought of lying between them. They were soft and limp, and seemed to cling to my body in a very disagreeable way. In fact, I was far more frightened in my bed, that night, than I had been on the road with the German shells overhead. However, I was not alone in the cellar, and that was a comfort: only a few feet away from my bed slept the lieutenant's orderly, a well-known character among American ambulance drivers who never called him anything else but Doucement, for reasons which I shall explain.

Doucement had kept a little wine-shop before the war, in some distant southern town. As a consequence, I suppose, he had become an incorrigible tippler, which did not prevent him from fighting like a lion at the battle of the Marne and later at Verdun. Indeed, he gave such an excellent report of himself for more than two years that, as a sort of reward, over and above the *croix de guerre*, he was sent from the hell of Douaumont to relatively quiet Neuvilly. His task was to ride with ambulance men and show them the way from the front to the different hospitals. We were all fond of him. He was a little man with a rubicund face, a bristly chin, and a broad and winning smile. His habitual tipsiness was a source of great merriment to all but never seemed to interfere with the carrying out of his duty.

It might have been thought that he enjoyed driving with us, but no, these expeditions were a nightmare to Doucement, who was otherwise so brave. This was due partly to our proverbially reckless driving, of which we were very proud, partly to the fact that, Doucement's brain being obscured by the enormous quantity of wine he absorbed every day, he never went out with us, but he saw imaginary dangers at every hand. He was terrified at the thought that we might overturn or drive into a ditch. Of course, we made the most of this situation and bounced him up and down at a shameless speed on shell-riddled roads. The poor man could do nothing but moan and wail: «*doucement!*» when he considered that his last hour had come.

The fear that he would be killed in a Ford driven by one of those fiendish Americans soon became a sort of obsession with him and even disturbed him in his sleep. Even if I had not been told about this, I would have found it out for myself that night. Not more than a few minutes had elapsed before my companion, who was in his usual happy state of mind when he turned in, began muttering to himself as he tossed on his stretcher. This went on for sometime, then the well-known cry rent the air: «*doucement!*»

It was impossible to sleep when Doucement had his familiar nightmare. All one could do was to wait until it came to a climax and the sufferer finally subsided. Waking him up was no help. He had to go through the whole process of being dumped into a ditch, and shaking him by the shoulder was simply postponing the agony by a few minutes. So I lay awake until, after much sighing and sobbing and a long succession of heartrending «*doucement*», the ex-wine merchant had met his death for the hundredth time in a Ford car. This done, he reposed more quietly and I gratefully closed my eyes.

Not for very long. Doucement's nightmare was bad enough, but a more elaborate one was soon to begin. In his conversation with me, before dinner, Lieutenant Jalin had incidentally remarked on the size of rats in this region of France.

'I believe,' he said, not without a certain amount of pride, 'I believe we have the largest rats in Europe.'

I soon discovered that he had not been boasting. There happened to be enough moonlight in our cellar to enable me to observe the size and shape of the huge rodents which I saw silhouetted against the walls as they came out of their holes. Doucement's wailing had kept them away for a while, but now that he had quieted down, they grew bolder and began running between our beds, looking for morsels of food. Some of these animals seemed to me as large as small dogs, and I could think of nothing else to do but draw my blanket (together with my winding-sheet) well over my head. This was not such a good idea, as the rats, seeing that they were undisturbed in their search for food, came closer to my bed and even ran over my body. I finally went to sleep because I was very tired and when one is tired at seventeen not even rats in an Argonne cellar can keep one awake.

The green lady

Towards the end of that summer[4], my father asked me in his quiet reasonable voice if I had any idea as to what I wanted to do. 'You are now twenty-two,' he added as if he were talking to

himself. He did not say, as many fathers would have done: 'At
your age I was already in business.' Or, 'What do you expect to
do for a living? When are you going to start working?' That was
not his manner. For the space of one half-minute, I wildly
agitated the question in my mind, then I answered: 'I am going
to be a painter.' 'A painter,' he repeated with polite interest.
'Then you must begin taking lessons. Hadn't you better ask
Henri[5] for advice?'

I did, not without blushing; it is always a little trying to tell a
fastidious artist, who believes that Da Vinci alone knew how to
draw, that one wishes to be an artist. But contrary to what I had
expected, Henri did not even smile. 'Go to the Grande-
Chaumière,' he said.

The Grande-Chaumière was a fair sized atelier in the street
of the same name, only a stone's throw from the famous
Rotonde.[6] I bought myself a green cardboard folder, some
papier Ingres, a couple of black pencils, and on a morning in
October nerved myself into entering the atelier. The room was
full of people and, much to my relief, no one paid the slightest
attention to me. I sat down and got my things ready. There was
a naked woman sitting on a platform where everybody could
see her, and although I thought her extremely plain I drew her
as carefully as I could. It was strange how quickly one felt at
ease in the atelier. Everybody worked hard and the sound of the
pencils on the paper was the only thing to be heard with the
exception of an occasional whisper. At the end of thirty
minutes, the model got up and stretched. Then she sat down in
another position, and I made another sketch of her bony
shoulders, large hips and heavy ankles. By the time I got up to
leave, I felt like a well seasoned *rapin* and strolled back to the
subway with quite a different view of the world.

That evening, my father took me with him to pay a call on his
friends the Steins who lived in the next street. Mr. Stein,
Gertrude Stein's brother, knew much about modern art and
owned a collection of paintings by Matisse who was then

achieving almost universal fame. 'My boy is going to study painting,' said my father as he introduced me. Oh, I wished he hadn't said that! Not in a drawing-room full of modern paintings which I was supposed to admire and did not know how to! Particularly terrifying was a lady with coal-like eyes and half of her face painted a bright apple green; nevertheless, there was something fascinating about her expression, half whimsical, half cruel, and the gay angle at which her funny 1905 hat was cocked.

'That's Mme Matisse,' said Mr. Stein, who saw I was looking at the picture. 'Nice, isn't she?'

He then told me that a gentleman, upon seeing this portrait in Matisse's studio, had asked the artist why he had painted the lady's face green. Whereupon Matisse gave the inquirer a piercing look and icily replied: 'Monsieur, her face is not green.'

My quarrel with Matisse was not that he had painted a lady's face green; Italian Primitives had done so before him. No, what distressed me was that I knew in my bones that I could never paint like him and that I had no desire even to try, although I would be expected to express myself more or less in the same language. 'Look at me,' the lady seemed to say. 'Forget about la Belle Ferronnière and her silly smooth cheeks. My face is crooked and half of it is green, and my nose well to one side as if I were sniffing at something. My blind eyes will not follow you around the room in the customary way, because I don't care whether you are in the room or not, but you will never forget me. I am crazy. I am the lady who sticks a long hat pin in her hat, zzzzzz! through the brain! I am modern, *mon garçon*. I am modern art, and you will come to me some day.'

'Well,' I thought, as I went home that evening, 'there you are. You have decided to be an artist in 1922, and in 1922 artists draw like Matisse who is undoubtedly a great painter, or like Picasso, who may be the Giotto of his century. You thought apples were round, but apples are really shaped like diamonds and you must draw them accordingly.'

So the next day, when I went back to the Grande-Chaumière and a naked lady sat down on the platform to be drawn, I gave her a rectangular head and rectangular hips. This was a depressing piece of work. Where curves are reasonably to be expected, I prefer curves and am not ashamed of saying so. Having therefore examined my drawing, I took my India rubber and erased one angle after another, neatly filling up the lines as I went along.

Henri, who also attended the Grande-Chaumière and happened to be there that morning, gave my sketch a glance and said nothing, although I fancied I saw his lips forming the dreaded word *«rondouillard»* as he saw the result of my efforts. Cubism was rampant in those days and anything like a rounded line was looked on with a sneer; this was a source of worry to me, because I could not train my eye to see people as an ensemble of articulated blocks. I suffered from a secret hankering after Greek art and in my heart of hearts placed Scopas and Praxiteles above any artist for the simple reason that they expressed to perfection my own ideal of beauty. This of course was a sin not to be confessed at a time when art was going wild and the «fauves» were roaring in art dealers' shops.

I have often thought that I would have been a different human being if, by some dispensation, I had never laid eyes on a Greek statue. A great many thoughts which lay dormant in me would probably not have awakened to life. The whole history of mankind repeats itself in most of us. We all go through a prehistoric age and medieval times; some of us develop into Renaissance men and women; not all of us reach modern times and it is only too clear to me that the greater part of humanity is at present still floundering in the dark ages.

I was just crawling out of what I might call my Gothic period when I first looked at a Greek statue, with other eyes than the eyes of childhood, and I felt at once conquered by an over-powering love of beauty. I felt very much the way a fifteenth-century student must have felt upon first viewing an antique torso freshly discovered in a ploughman's field, and I now dimly understood what the Fathers of the Church meant when they said that the gods and goddesses of Greece and Rome were devils exacting worship in the guise of superhuman beings. I was no more than a pagan returning to his sylvan deities.

All of which, I realized as I proceeded with my *rondouillard* sketch, could in no way be approved by the lady with the green face. She, I felt, would gladly have poked her umbrella through Mona Lisa's eye and with the same weapon have broken to small pieces the lovely collection of Greek terracottas in the Louvre. Yet, in my mind, she reigned supreme over modern art. I could see beauty in her wicked face, but not the kind of beauty which I wished to express, and here was a troublesome problem: did I have anything worth saying with a pencil? What I drew looked like what I might have drawn had I been living at the time of Prud'hon and David, so what good to me were Daumier, Cézanne and Matisse, all of whom I admired rather indiscriminately? Wasn't it rather absurd to go back when everyone was frantically rushing forward?

Months went by without helping me to solve my difficulties. I labored over my drawings and achieved some progress without ever turning out anything which might even remotely have put one in mind of modern art. I was so conscious of this that I amused myself by putting fancy dates at the bottom of my sketches, like January 1810, or September 1822. I don't think I ever reached 1900. 'Academic' would probably have been the word used by a critic, had he been allowed to examine my work, but I was careful not to show anyone what I did; above all, I took great pains to conceal my sketch-book from the fastidious Henri, who might have killed any ambition I had with a smile and a deadly remark.

On Keeping a Diary

Written in 1941, this text was delivered several times in the United States at various universities, including Princeton in 1941, and at Mills College, California, in 1944.

To keep a diary is a curious habit and we may well wonder why so many people cultivate it. What they are trying to do, I suppose, is to cause time to stand quite still, as if it were possible to keep time from rushing on by tracing thousands of tiny signs on a sheet of paper. They fancy that because they have noted the passing of a cloud in the sky or a few remarks exchanged by two or three people, time will respect these little things and not dump them into the big black hole of oblivion.

This, of course, is a delusion. If we could go to the very bottom of the question, after the manner of philosophers, we might discover that we are prompted to keep a diary by the apprehension of disappearing altogether. Hardly are we conscious of a fraction of time than it is already behind us. We cannot stop the present moment, but we feel somewhat comforted by the thought that in this perpetual and often alarming onrush of time, we have at least been able to establish a few landmarks. It flatters us. We are pleased with ourselves for rising above that implacable force which is dragging us along; we feel superior to it because we are conscious of it, we are not like animals in a freight car, conscious of nothing in their journey to the slaughterhouse. I grant you that is a small consolation, and I give it for what it is worth.

Considered from another angle, a diary is nothing more than a long letter which a man writes to himself. What kind of news does he give? Surely he can't give himself news of what he has done, seen and heard. He may even find it rather tiresome to give an account of his day, yet he keeps on, if he is a real diarist, because he still, secretly, expects news. News of himself. The most curious part about it all is that he usually succeeds in getting it.

After a few years of journal writing, he realizes that there was a slight mist over the mirror, and now the mist has evaporated and he sees himself a little better. This is not always a pleasant sight. Nevertheless, our diarist would rather know. He is more

accurately informed as to the kind of person he is; he is
disillusioned, but wiser. Above all, he is more acutely conscious
of living. He is unable to ward off death, but he can immensely
increase his awareness of life.

We have all experienced that feeling of discomfort caused by a
lapse of memory. To forget the name of a person we know, of a
place where we have spent several days, what, at times, can be
more irritating? That, however, is not exactly what I mean. If
the fact of forgetting a name, a word or a date can nettle us, we
are far more disturbed by a lapse of memory of which we
ourselves are the object, not as regards others, but as regards
ourselves. A certain degree of anxiety is involved in lapses of
our own memory which have to do with our past. To be unable
to recall what we were doing at such and such a moment of our
life may be very disagreeable: we feel that those days, or weeks,
for which we cannot very well account have, as it were, been
stolen from us. Our mind has proved incapable of retaining the
whole mass of our memories. There must be a rift in the bag,
and we are as puzzled and as worried as a miser who feels that
his wealth is slipping away from him. Where were we? What
were we doing in such and such a month? What kind of
thoughts did I have then? We must be capable of answering
these questions in a general way at least, otherwise, in some
secret part of our brain, a fear will arise, one of the most subtle
fears in the world, the fear of losing one's memory.

There is a saying of Bergson's which never fails to strike me
whenever I think of it, because it always seems new and there is
always some part of it which is yet unexplored: 'Consciousness
is memory.' It would seem difficult to say more in fewer words.
We can fully exist only inasmuch as we remember. Hence that
almost superstitious guarding of our memory. We do not want

our memory to slumber, because we fear the lessening of consciousness which that would entail. From childhood to middle age, we want the whole of our being to remain present without any interruption.

Finally comes the day when the fight is no longer possible and exhausted memory ends by giving in. It is true, nevertheless, that, by one of those mysterious freaks of our brain, which we still know imperfectly, childhood memories are apt to rise again at that very time, in the dusk, but that is not a very good sign either. The glow at the end of our life does not compensate for the shadows which now dim the features of the youthful face, once our own. When that time comes, let us open our diary, if we have been wise or foolish enough to keep a diary: by the magic of the written word, everything is given back to us for a little while, our young days and the hopes that accompanied them, the sky above Paris or Rome, the woods through which we have walked, the libraries where we used to work, all the places where we have weighed our chances of a happy life and struggled to build our future. For the space of a few hours, time has stopped and that which can never come back has taken the place of the present in a sort of mirage which gives us a pang.

After all, it may not be in nature's intentions for us to remember everything and I wonder if forgetfulness is not a blessing in disguise. Ten or twelve years ago, in a rash and peremptory way, I wrote that death was primarily a complete and absolute loss of all memory. I would no longer say such a thing, but the person I then was found it difficult to admit that the landmarks along the road should ever disappear under the snow which inevitably covers our footsteps. The reason why we know ourselves so badly is that we can never see ourselves very well, except in the light of the present. We can only very imperfectly imagine what we are going to be like in the future. At the very thought of the old man he will be some day, a young man takes violent exception. If, in a magic mirror, he were able to see the various personages that will represent him as he treads downward, he might feel very angry, or very sad. 'Who,' he would ask, 'is that funny little man with a red face and no hair at all, writing at a desk?' 'Why, that's you.' 'And who may that despondent old fellow be, walking alone in a deserted alley and turning over the dead leaves with the end of his stick?' 'Don't ask. That is you again.'

But what the young man might not know is that the middle-aged man with the red face is perhaps quite reconciled to his lot and no doubt happy, whereas the old gentleman who seems despondent may be only indifferent to the world, and in his own way quite contented.

So it may be possible to reread one's diary with a certain amount of philosophical detachment and even with a certain pleasure. It all depends on circumstances. Perhaps it is wiser not to turn back the leaves of an old diary at a time of moral distress, remembering the famous lines of Dante, which I shall not quote. In a general way, however, to keep and to reread one's diary can prove only beneficial to a writer. For one thing, it will make him more attentive to what is going on around him as well as to the many phases of his inner life. The world around us is constantly, if mutely, begging us to look at it, but many go through it as if they were deaf and blind. Of them might be said what the psalmist says of pagan idols: that they have ears and do not hear, eyes and they do not see. The man who keeps a diary quickly forms the habit of observing and of listening, in order to write down what he has seen and heard as accurately as possible in his little book. Instinctively, if he is a writer, he will discard what is unimportant (even though it may seem important at the time) and make a note of what will be of greatest interest in the future (although it may seem trivial at the moment he sets it down). So much intellectual wealth is at his disposal that it can hardly be reckoned, for memory is, after all, mainly a question of paying proper attention, and what we forget in spite of the efforts we make to direct our attention our diary will remember for us, but no better epigraph can be found for a diary than these words of a Hindu philosopher: an inattentive man is a dead man.

The trouble about keeping a diary is that it is impossible to say everything. Stevenson once wrote: 'There are not words enough in all Shakespeare to express the merest fraction of a man's experience in an hour.' If you doubt it, just try to make a note of what goes through your mind in the space of a minute. It cannot very well be done, for the simple reason that thought goes infinitely faster than words, particularly written words. You will remember two or three things which are more striking than the rest, but the thread is soon lost and with it a certain number of accessory thoughts.

One question which I am constantly asking myself when I read a diary (and there are few books I find more entertaining than a good diary) — one question which amounts almost to an obsession is: What else happened in the author's life on that particular day? What else did he say or do which he does not tell us? What else did he think which he himself has forgotten? A page in a diary is like a door that opens ever so little three or four hundred times so that we can finally form an approximate idea of what goes on in that secret room: the author's brain.

Such is the drawback of that kind of literature. It almost always leaves us with a sensation of hunger, nor is that the fault of the man who keeps a diary. There would not be enough paper in the world, nor enough time in a human life, to say everything we might want to know. I say that it almost always leaves us with an unsatiated appetite, because there is, after all, Pepys's diary, but it does not extend over a period of more than nine years. Even so, however full his diary may be, there are many gaps in it which irritate our curiosity. It isn't because that worthy person didn't try to say everything, but he never suspected that we should some day be prying into his secrets; he wrote for himself, not for us, and there are many things which he fails to set down, much, we feel, to our loss.

When I was about twenty, I took it into my mind to keep a

diary myself, but I wanted it to be a diary in every way more complete than any diary I had yet held in my hands; my ambition was to put in it everything one can reasonably put in a diary. With that plan in mind and by way of stimulating my zeal, I wrote the first page on a very large sheet of paper, which was really a piece of wrapping paper; it was so large that it covered most of my writing table; moreover, I delighted in writing as small as possible. For two or three days, I put down scrupulously everything I saw and heard and as much as I could of what went on inside my head. I need hardly say that I did not go very far, to begin with, because it was so tiring and also because what I had to say did not always strike me as being very interesting; but what really stopped me and put an end to that particular diary was that I was so busy writing it that I no longer had time to live. Unfortunately, I destroyed this document, a clumsy attempt to say the whole truth and nothing but the truth. I should have liked to reread those pages. What appeared trivial and commonplace in 1922, how curious it might seem to me in 1941! I did not then know what one might call the optics of diaries. I did not realize that what seems trite or dull in the present undergoes in time an essential transformation and may turn into something rare and singular.

That is one of the secrets of a good diary. You think that you have nothing to say, you fancy that only people who lead interesting lives should keep diaries, but what life is not interesting in some respect? A diary is the book which can be written by those who do not believe that they are writers, and there is no reason why such a book should not be a great book and attract thousands of readers, if it is sincere, if it is accurate, and if it delivers itself properly of its message. A man who writes 'I am alone, and because I am alone, I am unhappy' finds an echo among all the lonely souls in this world, and you may be sure that there are quite a few. I said a while ago that a diary was like a letter which he writes to thousands of unknown friends. Such a letter does not always get an answer, but it comforts many a man or woman who feels the heaviness of life. It is something of a consolation to be able to think: 'The person who wrote that has had the same experience as I. We have gone through the same difficult moments, we have been annoyed, and irritated and disappointed by the same things. I am therefore not alone.'

The three main requisites for a good diary, a diary worthy of the name, are first, sincerity, then accuracy, and finally the faculty of choosing what is important and rejecting what is unimportant.

The problem of sincerity in a diary is such a tremendous one that it would alone form the subject matter of a complete book. It goes without saying that one is bound to speak the truth in keeping a diary. Indeed, one wishes to speak the truth, and it is because one wishes to speak the truth that one keeps a diary. But at the very start we are held up. We are quite willing to make our own confession, but is it permissible to make other people's confessions as well as ours, and how is this to be avoided when our life is mixed up with the lives of ten or twenty people? In order to tell of such-and-such incident in my life, I shall have to explain the part played by So-and-So in that same incident, and should So-and-So ever read what I have written, how angry, or how sad, he or she may be! Let us, therefore, replace his name by initials and in case the diary should ever be printed, let us indicate the necessary cut. Obviously, if it weren't for laws on libel, we should have better diaries. It is not always the fear of hurting his neighbor which guides the diarist in these matters, but simply the fear of being prosecuted. Be that as it may, he is compelled to give us a fragmentary picture. Unfortunately, a half-truth is very often a sort of distant cousin of falsehood; a half-truth may give a false impression which nothing but the missing half could correct. You see what slippery ground we are treading. If the author is really sincere (and sincerity is a gift in literature, a gift not bestowed upon all) — if the author is sincere, he will cut out the whole passage

rather than allow a half-truth to be printed which might
mislead his reader. But, of course, by not mentioning the
incident in question, by remaining silent, he may still be telling
an untruth. This evil deed which I committed and which I
cannot mention, that is, in detail, because it might get So-and-
So into trouble, I refuse to tell the reader about it in a few
skillfully 'doctored' lines which might lead him to believe me a
better person than I really am. I don't want him to think: 'How
honestly this man accuses himself!' So the writer takes his
scissors and cuts out the part about his evil deed. Is the reader
aware of this operation? Not in the least. What then has become
of that much-talked-about sincerity? I could not tell you. I see it
nowhere. It must have gone out for a walk whilst the writer was
playing with his scissors.

As for accuracy, I need hardly point out that it is indispensable in a diary. Not so long ago, in an American novel about
Paris, I read the description of a certain street which I know
well. The author described the elms which he fancied he had
seen in that place. This bothered me a little, because there are
no elms there, but plane trees, plane trees which I think of as
old friends of mine. I believe that if that novelist had kept a
diary, he might have been more observant. The mistake he
made was, of course, of little importance. To mistake a plane
tree for an elm matters very little in a novel. It is a much more
serious matter for a diarist to give us an inaccurate account of a
conversation he has heard.

When the Goncourt diaries came out, Ernest Renan
protested vigorously against some statements which he was
supposed to have made in the presence of Edmond de Goncourt. He said he had been completely misunderstood, and he
very broadly hinted that Goncourt was not capable of understanding what he, Renan, had said. Somehow, it would seem
that Goncourt was right, as the words he gives as Renan's are
too much like Renan himself to have been invented. They don't
show Renan in a very favorable light, and it is never very

pleasing to be confronted with one's own words in black and white, particularly when those words have been spoken without much reflection.

This reminds me of something which happened to me at the time I was bringing out the first volume of my own diary. Having in mind the controversy between Goncourt and Renan, I had made it a rule never to say anything about anyone, in my printed diary, without having first shown certain passages to the people whom they concerned. Now I had come to a page in which I mentioned a well-known Parisian actress. She had great intellectual gifts and her conversation was a source of delight to many writers who appreciated her wit and her unfailing sense of the right word. That day she talked of the impression she made on the public whenever she appeared on the stage. She told me what the public thought of her and what she thought of the public, and what she had to say she said in a few sentences which her talent made unforgettable: terse, ferociously worded sentences. Directly I came home, that day, I wrote down what she had said and thought no more of it. Years went by and a publisher asked me for my diary. Having agreed to give it to him, I copied it, in part, and had not turned many of its leaves before I came to my conversation with this lady. I immediately called her up, mindful of Goncourt and Renan, and read her the whole passage that concerned her. It was a little ingenuous on my part, I grant you. The lady listened, she listened very well, and then asked me if I was sure she had said all that. I said I was. She was far too courteous to contradict me, but she suggested that I change her words somewhat, and she even obliged me with a little speech which, she thought, might take the place of what she had said a few years before: it was a very clever little speech, but I mourned for the marvelous vitriolic statement which I had noted before. I listened and took down the words which she would have preferred to have said; they were never printed: I cut out the whole page.

The third requisite in keeping a good diary is a gift for discriminating between the many things which life is constantly thrusting upon us. This gift of discrimination is nothing else but talent. Only the clumsiest of writers lack this ability to choose, and say everything. It may be objected that the very fact that the writer makes a choice among the things he wishes to say indicates that truth has once more undergone an operation. To choose is necessarily to eliminate, to prune. So it looks as if we were again going to flounder in the problem of literary sincerity, but I do not think so. I believe, on the contrary, that a writer knows perfectly well when he is being truthful and when not, and just how much he must say in order to remain truthful; that is, in fact, a part of his talent.

Having made all these preliminary remarks, I should now like to say a few words on some of the diaries which seem best to illustrate my theory of what one might call the ideal diary. An ideal diary should at once be introspective and objective, or, if you prefer words a little less barbarous, it should allow the reader to see what is going on inside as well as outside the writer's brain.

We shall not dwell very long on the Goncourt diaries, as they are too well known. They are among the most interesting diaries ever written and indeed it seems impossible to have an accurate idea of literary life in nineteenth-century France unless one has read them. They are not complete and will not be published *in extenso* for some time yet, but we have already nine volumes which cover almost all of the second half of the nineteenth century. A half-century of anecdotes, of gossip, of scraps of conversations, but also of literary experience, of endless trouble taken over books which we no longer read. We should, to be fair, add that one volume at least, the fourth, is a most valuable historical document on the Franco-Prussian War of 1870 and the Commune. There we no longer have literary small talk but a very dramatic chapter of French history. Renan, as I mentioned earlier, disliked this diary and accused its author of lacking what he called *des idées générales*, a quite unforgivable sin in his eyes and a way of hinting that the Goncourts had no sense. Be that as it may, we can safely say that philosophical speculations had little attraction for the Goncourts. To use a favorite phrase of Gautier's, they were men for whom the external world existed, and from the point of view of the inner life, their diaries are singularly meager. The life of the soul, all that interior world which we carry within us, did not interest them in the least. For that reason, probably, those otherwise fascinating volumes leave us with a sensation of emptiness, or of what Ecclesiastes would call vanity.

The contrary excess, I mean an exaggerated attention given to what goes on in us, produces that enormous, that monstrous, document known as *Amiel's Journal*. The manuscript comprises almost 17,000 pages, which means that, if it were published in its entirety, it would fill forty-eight volumes. Three or four only have been printed. You remember that Amiel was a professor who fancied that he was called to be a great man and to do great things, great things which remained a little hazy in his mind and which he himself never indicated very clearly. During thirty years of his life he tirelessly made notes of the smallest aspects of his intellectual activities and of his moral problems. Once in a while he threw a hasty glance in the direction of that external world which the Goncourts loved so passionately, but Amiel's glances were never those of a man who really knew how to use his eyes. He had little sense of the picturesque. Like Samson Agonistes, he had become the dungeon of himself. Ideas, books, his differences of opinion from year to year and also his sentimental setbacks are the main themes of his magnum opus (Goodness knows it is magnum). I do not say that his diary is devoid of interest. It is exactly suited to certain introspective temperaments, but most of us tire of it rather early in the day. He was intelligent and morbidly sensitive, and we end by asking ourselves what use his eyes and his ears could have been to such a man if not to throw him back within himself with an irresistible force. His perpetual dissatisfaction with himself and with the world is at times very moving, and because any form of human suffering is worthy of attention and respect, but, at the present moment, I am hunting that rare animal, the perfect diary, and I wonder who is going to give it to us.

In 1935 Jules Renard's diary was published, but compared with Amiel's diary it is nothing more than a pamphlet: 860 pages long. It goes from the year 1887 to the year 1910. I can't say that Renard is one of my favorite authors, but he has something to say, in his diary, and he says it with minute accuracy. He was a narrow-minded man, a bitter man, and, when occasion offered, an apparently heartless man; however, like a great many heartless people, he had sudden fits of emotion and sensibility when other people were nice to him. To be sure, he did not belong to the same race as Amiel, and it would seem almost comical to compare them, but he was far more entertaining, if it is entertainment we desire. He was cold to the point of iciness, but sometimes not quite so cold as he would like us to believe. I believe there was some degree of affectation in his cruelty, and he was certainly guided by a desire to see things as they are. Above all, he despised those who tried to make him take a hawk for a handsaw. Unfortunately, as often happens to skeptics, he was apt to take handsaws for hawks without any encouragement from others. His intentions were good, and as far as we know, he was sincere. Yet his horror of sentiment sometimes confused his judgement and he spoke harshly of what was closest to his heart, but then he did not realize that his sincerity was deviating somewhat; he would have mistaken this for modesty, or reserve, or a sense of decency. For example, when he describes his father's death. His father killed himself accidentally with a shotgun. Here is the description of that event, a good example of impassibility in the Stendhal tradition:

'I go into the courtyard and say to Marinette who picked up Mother from off the ground: "It's all over. Come." She enters, straight and very pale, looks sideways in the direction of the bed. She is unable to cry. She says, thinking of her mother: "Keep her from entering. She is distracted." We remain, both of us. He is there [that is, Renard's father], stretched out on his back, mouth and eyes open. Between his legs, his gun and his walking-stick. His hands are still warm, not clenched. Just above the waist line, a dark spot, something like a small fire that has gone out.'

And that is all. Two days later the funeral takes place. 'I think that everyone is watching me,' says Renard, 'and that after my father, I am the most important person in the ceremony.' At the cemetery he lingers a little in front of the grave. 'People are beginning to move away,' he writes, 'but I stay on. I stay on. Ah, wretched actor that I am! I feel that I am doing it a little on purpose.'

Ten or twelve days later we have this curious entry: 'Sometimes, by a macabre sort of imitation, I stop in the middle of the road and open my mouth as he opened his when he lay on his bed.'

Here, of course, we are confronted with a desire to speak the truth carried to the point of brutality. What Renard fears most is to be taken in, and he won't be taken in any more by himself than by anyone else. He certainly knows how to see and how to make his reader see what he sees.

Here, for instance, is a portrait of the great painter Toulouse-Lautrec, who was, as you know, a dwarf: 'Lautrec, a tiny blacksmith with a pince-nez on his nose. A small bag with two compartments in which he inserts his legs. Thick lips. He often mentions small men as if to say: "I am not so small as all that." His smallness makes a painful impression, at first. But then he is so alert, so pleasant, with a grunt that separates his sentences and raises his lips, just as a draught that raises the pads on a door.'

Elsewhere he mentions the writer Marcel Schwob and notes 'the blinking of Schwob's eyelids when he is telling a lie.'

Or this about Mallarmé, whom he sees in a theater lobby during an intermission: 'Mallarmé the faun slips deftly through the crowd, trembling lest he be finally understood.'

Where Renard is at his best is when he makes very brief observations which remind one of the Japanese haikai, homely or comical haikai, not devoid, however, of a certain poetic quality. For example, he sees a red rug hanging from a window and he says that the house is sticking out its tongue. Or he looks at sunbeams going through a mass of clouds, and it reminds him of knitting needles in a ball of wool. He loves to observe animals and sees them not only with great accuracy but with an almost unfailing sense of humor. The flight of pigeons puts him in mind of young girls smothering their laughter. He looks at a pig and notes that pigs wear their caps over their eyes. And he looks at human beings, too, with the same impartiality, perhaps with a lesser degree of sympathy. His diary is full of thumbnail sketches, many of which are fraught with cruelty. Loti, Goncourt, Edmond Rostand, with his moustache and his monocle, all the wax dolls of the period form a sort of procession in front of us. There are also an enormous number of anecdotes and witty sayings, most of them vitriolic. He goes out of his way to seem unkind; once more, he doesn't want to be taken in by himself. He writes: 'It is not sufficient to be happy. One must feel that one's neighbor is in trouble.' Having read this bulky volume, we close it with a feeling of dissatisfaction. We feel as if we had passed through a world of pygmies, where even the great men of the time are stunted, and that is inherent in the personality of the man who saw them thus.

We now come to a man of infinitely greater value. Let us open the *Copybooks* in which Maurice Barrès reported on what he had seen and heard. Here we are in the presence of an exceptional intellect at the service of a great and lofty personality. This gentleman, whose ugliness is so peculiar, with his large hooked nose, with a long wisp of hair sweeping across his forehead and with that melancholy expression which makes him look like a despondent bird, is one of the very few writers who really tower above their time and know how to speak intelligibly to the generations that follow. I am aware of all that can be said against him, but there are in his thought what a mathematician might call invariants which are as valid today as they were twenty or forty years ago. Above all, there is his conception of France and of the indispensable character of French civilization. This, however, is just a parenthesis which I hasten to close, because the purely patriotic portion of his works, honorable though it be, is not the best from a literary point of view. Personally, I think him more interesting in his singularities than when he addresses the millions of subscribers to the *Echo de Paris*.[7] Despite his tremendous literary reputation, which can be explained, partly, by fashion and politics, he wrote for the happy few, and the fewer they were, the better Barrès seemed to write. Stretching this point, we might say that he never wrote better than when he wrote for himself, when he wrote for that ego which he was weak enough to adore. *Le culte du moi*, the cult of the ego, what a sad sound that phrase has and how cramped one feels in that formula! It was the formula in which the great writer chose to enclose himself, and yet what else is a diary but one aspect of that melancholy cult? However, we must not quarrel with him on that score since that error in perspective gave us a document of considerable interest.

In the ten or twelve volumes of Barrès's diary, there are many pages which we no longer read, pages which are no longer read except by the specialists of French interior politics. His accounts of parliamentary sessions hold our attention only when they deal with questions that will forever be actual, such as the fate of the French nation, and we quickly turn the pages that tell us of nothing but questions propounded by a dead parliamentarian to dead parliamentarians. But there are other things, too, and nowhere can be found portraits drawn by a more masterful hand, nor by a hand more delicate in its extraordinary firmness. One has to go back to Victor Hugo, the

Victor Hugo of *Choses vues*, to find the equivalent of such portraits, or even to Saint-Simon. Before quoting one or two passages which, I believe, will justify our admiration for Barrès, I feel it necessary to say a few words on the enormous part played by the dead in his intellectual life. Side by side with the cult of the ego, there was the cult of the dead. He tells us himself that he was enamored of death, and indeed I find it difficult to open his *Copybooks* without tripping over a great many funeral wreaths. This is one of the least known traits of the Latin races. Anglo-Saxons have a very different point of view. They may think of death, but they are unwilling to dwell on the subject and to mention it unless they have to. There is a tendency in them not to emphasize the fact that we all have to go. Not so the Latins. Nowhere more than in France do funerals assume the dramatic grandeur that seems a heritage of former times, although this spirit of pomp has somewhat abated in recent years. Up to 1920 or thereabout, a French funeral put one in mind of the fifteenth-century Italian pictures of what was termed the Triumph of Death. The dead were not hurried from church to cemetery as they are now. They were very slowly taken to their resting place in huge hearses drawn by horses that were magnificently caparisoned in black and silver and that bore nodding ostrich plumes on their heads. I remember how, as a child, I was awed to the point of alarm by this, to me, terrifying spectacle.

Jules Renard, who liked funerals almost as much as Barrès did, has given us a picture of Barrès at Verlaine's funeral. 'Barrès,' he writes, 'has just the voice that is needed to speak at someone's grave, with tones worthy of a crow.' Let us listen to that voice for a moment in a description of a funeral in a small French town, Charmes-sur-Moselle:

'The bells are ringing: the dead man is going to be taken from his home. How they are silent: the service has begun. The dogs continue to play, the stonecutters to cut their stones, and the women to talk. But half an hour later, the bells once more raise their voices and the procession leaves the church. As it goes forth, it causes the town noises to abate and to cease. It makes a black spot which spreads over Main Street. Everyone turns his head and looks back on his days of sorrow. First comes the tread of feet, then the liturgical murmur, then, below my windows, the church candles and the purple surplices. The choirboy heads the procession with the lofty cross which he holds in both hands and rubs against his itching nose. In the middle, a clatter of hoofs: the omnibus horse drawing the hearse. Tall top hats and black frock-coats come next. The accent of Lorraine floating above all conversations. To end up, a group of women, a Pietà: the widow and her daughters, the sisters from the poor house, the butcher's wife, the grocer's wife, in their Sunday best, but already bearing in their faces the disease of which they will die.

The little procession has gone by; a stone has slipped under the water. I have described the outer aspect of the scene, the small respectable scene; but what lies underneath? The little town has resumed its work, sawing wood, cutting stones, getting its dinner ready, and riding bicycles.'

Barrès's style has been compared (much to his own delight) to a fish drawn out of the water and going through a gamut of exquisite colors before it dies. What one finds, in that diary, apart from men and women vigorously portrayed, is the portrait of Maurice Barrès himself. One may not like him, one may actively dislike him, as André Gide professes to dislike him, but even if one later recants any feeling of admiration for him, it is difficult not to appreciate the quality of an intellect so marvelously varied in its aspects. This singular person tells us that 'more and more, when he is alone, does he find it impossible to escape from the misty romance of death. By slow degrees,' he goes on, 'I am putting this romance into my life.' With ineffable pleasure he loses himself in what he calls barren but inexhaustible reveries. The same man, however, wishes to lead an active life, that is, to play a part in the political life of France. At Elsinore, no doubt, he would have tried to bring about the king's death, but he might have preferred to that consummation the exquisite torment of doubt and the agonies of a diseased will. Far be it for me to draw a parallel between him and Hamlet. He himself would have protested as any man of his temperament would protest against a precise definition of his personality, but there is between the two a certain degree of relationship, and when I hear him being criticized and sometimes reviled, I cannot help thinking that, in the eyes of Fortinbras, Hamlet was no doubt little more than a neurotic, but that Fortinbras himself was something of a brute.

André Gide's dislike of Barrès is founded, as one might have supposed, on very intelligent reasons. One can readily see what Gide, who has always been so enthusiastically in love with life, could find to criticize in intellectual pleasures whose principal object is death.

Since I have mentioned Gide, I should like to say a few words about his diary. This book, a moderately long book of about twelve-hundred pages, deserves a thorough examination. Gide's diary is important first of all because of its author's position in modern French literature. But even had Gide written nothing else but this diary, it would still retain much of its value as a literary document, as a testimonial. That word *testimonial* is very characteristic of Gide, who uses it very often. He is, in his own eyes, the witness of his truth, and it is to that truth which he purposed to bear witness in his diary. The book begins in the last years of the nineteenth century. The last pages take us to the days preceding the present world war. So we are in a position to see Gide in his youth, in his middle age and as an old man.

Indeed, he gives us a remarkable portrait of himself. Not only the portrait of a writer, but the portrait of a man the equivalent of which I have never yet seen, because it is the portrait of a man who, so far, has successfully resisted all attempts to analyze his personality. As we close the book, a book in which he tells us just as much as he wishes us to know, and he wishes us to know a good deal, the reader, the unprejudiced reader, as Gide would call him, is justified in asking himself: 'Well, what kind of man is he? What is he made of? What does he think? What does he believe? He is always telling us what he thinks. How is it that when we fancy we know him, he is perpetually escaping us? We think we hold him and he is already far off.' This impression is far from incorrect. No one has ever gone through intellectual variations with such deftness as Gide. But here is an even more disconcerting fact about him: his longing for absolute sincerity drives him from contradiction to contradiction, and yet he gives us an impression of indomitable firmness.

'I have brushed past everything,' he one day said, and I believe that sentence depicts him as much as any sentence can depict such a complex personality. Like all great writers, Gide has his legend. That is to say, his friends as well as his foes have tried to grasp him by simplifying him. They have wasted their time. On one occasion, speaking of a word portrait of him by a rather well-known author, he remarked: 'All those who do not know me think it an excellent likeness.'

The following excerpt from his diary will enable us to catch a glimpse of Gide as he really is. We will see how careful he is to tell the truth about himself as accurately, and as humbly, as possible. The entry is dated 1935. It refers to a visit he received from a refugee, probably a German who came to him for advice, and no doubt for a little money.

'He arrives just as I am about to go out. I have an appointment with the dentist, I am already late. No one to answer the door and say that Mr. Gide is not in. I come, tying my shoe strings. The refugee embarks on an interminable story to explain that his case should interest me particularly. Out of a leather satchel, he produces an album containing already many signatures of celebrated people, requests me to add mine; I detest that sort of thing. He hears me sniffle and thinks he is being very nice by exclaiming: "Have you caught cold?" He

would like to arouse my pity, but I haven't the time to be
moved. "Come back another day. Don't you see that today I
can't ..." "I came yesterday already." Now that he has me, he
wants to make the most of it. This is very clumsy of him. He
succeeds only in irritating me. He senses that and wastes a little
more time apologizing. All the hope he had placed in my
advice, in my help, in my assistance, vanishes. His voice
quavers, he fumbles for words ...

'And all day long, I am hounded by remorse, for my insufficient aid, for my abruptness, for my impatience. If only I had
made a note of that unhappy man's address, as I usually do.
But no; there is no way of making amends.

'Unbearable *moral sensation* of deficiency, of indigence (I am
the indigent one).'

How difficult it is to write such a page as that one, and what a
strict regard for intellectual honesty it implies! Here we have
not the shadow of a feint. If there is any skill in the passage, it
simply means that the absence of any kind of skill is probably
skill in a supreme degree. If talking about oneself is one of the
most fascinating occupations in a writer's life, it can also be one
of the most hazardous, because it involves the whole of a man's
personality, good and bad.

An Experiment in English

Originally published in *Harper's Magazine*
in September 1941.

One of the most curious consequences of the present state of affairs in Europe is the problem which now faces a great many men and women who have been driven from their homes by the invader and have sought refuge in this country. A strange and unforeseen problem: these people have been told by fate that, if they wish to live, they must learn English.

At first this would not seem very disturbing. To learn English, why yes. Millions of foreigners have learned English: it isn't anything like a feat, it is simply a question of time and patience and hard work. If some of us were told that, owing to almost unimaginable circumstances, we had to learn, let us say, Portuguese to go on living, we should no doubt accept the bargain; we might even, at first, think it a little funny, rather exciting, but as time wore on, our opinion on this matter might undergo a change.

It is all very well to take French or German or Italian in college, they are a part of our studies; but in all probability our knowledge of those languages will seldom go beyond a sort of theoretical stage. We may be able to recite one or two of La Fontaine's fables, which, by the way, is extremely difficult to do well, or we may be able to write a letter with no grammatical mistakes, provided the letter is not too long; but even if we can't, well, it won't matter very much; should we get our irregular verbs a little wrong, there will still be room for happiness in our lives, whereas a refugee's happiness might be greatly interfered with by an insufficient knowledge of English.

Let us go back to the almost unbelievable time when there was no war. People lived in their homes and were reasonably happy. They did not stop to ask themselves whether they were happy or not, nor do we. A certain amount of boredom goes into the composition of the average happiness, latent, not conscious boredom, a strange feeling that, although the years rush along, the days are apt to lag. Some years ago a French play was given, the hero of which was a man whose life was a series of minor worries: his cook gave notice on the eve of a dinner party, or his wife had a row with his best friend, or his secretary ran away. One day something really went wrong and there was cause for tears, scenes, and some of those words which, once said, can never be unsaid. Finally differences were adjusted and the tense atmosphere of drama gave way to that of peace. 'Well,' said someone, as the hero sank into an armchair, 'everything is all right now. Happiness is here.' Whereupon the hero, with the face of a man who has been badly harried by life and is a little skeptical of certain words, looked gloomily at the audience and said: 'Happiness? Well, I'll get used to it ...'

Now precisely that kind of happiness with its monotony and complete lack of excitement is what the world is pining for today. It was taken away suddenly from millions of men and women in the fall of 1939 and only then could they appreciate what they had lost. With their country defeated and hope killed in their hearts, some of them preferred to face a long exile rather than live under the rule of the invader. So they came to this country, where freedom is still to be found, and with them, to be sure, they brought their language.

Most of them had little else to bring, but a man's language is so very much his own property that he almost identifies himself with it. This is a characteristic human trait. We are inclined to consider that what belongs to us and what we cherish most is somehow a part of ourselves. Our worth, our moral value, depend largely on the value of that very thing which we wish to make our own. A miser is, or believes he is, so dependent on his wealth that without it he does not think that he can live, because, in his subconscious mind, it has become a part of himself; and he is really a very poor man. An art collector feels pretty much the same way towards his pictures: they do not belong to him as much as he belongs to them, and if they are destroyed by fire, for instance, his own soul is scorched by the flames. The same appears to be true of any kind of attachment, from the lowest to the highest forms of love. We are what we love most. All of us have met intellectuals who had obviously shed their humanity and transformed themselves into books, and that great modern thinker, Leonardo da Vinci, tells us in his brutal way that the average man is no more than a digestive apparatus.

Now, language is a part of us to such a point that we are not even conscious of it except under unusual circumstances. It is of course a property which we share with millions of other people, but it is nevertheless so essentially a part of us that if, in some inconceivable way, it were taken from us completely, almost every form of mental process might come to a halt in our brain. Try to think for only a few seconds without the help of words and see how far you can get.

I know of a French child — it would take a French child to do this — who once asked his mother the following question: 'Mother, when you think do you think thoughts or do you think words?' Whereupon the mother immediately answered: 'Don't be absurd, child. When you think, you think thoughts of course.' But as she was an intelligent woman with a reflective turn of mind, she began wondering at her own answer. What did it mean to think thoughts and not words? So she asked a friend of hers who taught philosophy in Paris, and he said to her: 'You had better tell your little boy that we don't know.'

Well, I don't know any more than that philosopher, but it seems to me that we can't very well have thoughts without words, although I am positive that many times a day we are treated to words without thought. When I was younger and knew even less about such matters than I do today, I used to be irritated by a certain question which was sometimes asked me; later I found out that when we are irritated by a question it often means that we have not understood it. The question was: 'Do you think in English or in French?' My answer was: 'Tell me first if we think in words,' with the unexpressed assumption that we didn't. Usually I obtained no reply and felt in consequence very superior. Nevertheless, the question that had been asked me was interesting and my answer, at best, a display of ignorance.

We may take it for granted that practically all our thinking is done in terms of a definite language. A language is not only a means of designating objects or describing emotions; it is in itself a process of thought. When the Latin mind was confronted with a certain aspect of the universe, it created certain words to express it. This same aspect of the universe apprehended by the Anglo-Saxon race received a different name. The phenomenon described was essentially the same whatever name it happened to be called, but the difference in the names argued a difference in the mentalities of the two races.

The French language interprets the universe in one way, the English language in another; it is the same universe seen from different angles. There is, I believe, a letter written by Keats in which the poet explains that some thoughts expressed in his poems were suggested to him by words. To a student of poetry this of course is an invaluable indication, but many a prose writer has experienced also the power of words to create thought. It sometimes happens that the very words used to express a thought cause it to deviate into an entirely unforeseen channel, nor does this argue a loose mode of thinking. To be sure, a philosopher or a mathematician will not allow himself to be lured away from his path by the magic of words, but to a poet, or even to a novelist, this deviation may prove a godsend, a source of real inspiration. We may be tolerably certain that had Keats been born French he might have written a poem called *Endymion* but the contents of that poem would have been different. To put it in other words, a French translation of *Endymion* as we know it can in no wise represent what Keats would have written had he written in French instead of English, because the mere sound of French words would have suggested an entirely different set of images.

A language is a world from which it is very difficult to escape. Yet to many in recent months it has become a necessity to give up their language and adopt a new and difficult means of expressing themselves. Some are succeeding better than others: it depends on age and natural gifts; the young are quicker in adapting themselves to circumstances; the old — well, an old man in exile is always in a bad plight.

Having lived in Paris for many years, it has been my good fortune to meet most of the important present-day writers of France. A few are in this country, and as I am studying the problem of learning to think in a new language, I shall mention here the case of a man who is well known in most countries of Europe as one of the greatest exponents of modern thought[8]. We have been friends for fifteen or sixteen years. He had been in America for several months when the catastrophe of June 1940 made his return to Paris impossible. Upon my arrival in this country, towards the middle of last summer, I went to see him. We had a great deal to say to each other and a great many questions to ask. He wanted to know what was happening in his country, how his friends were faring, who was alive and who was missing. We spoke French of course. Unlike many philosophers, he has an exquisite sense of the beauty of words and expresses himself with the preciseness and the simplicity of a real artist. For that and other reasons I have always enjoyed listening to him, and I have never left him without feeling that in some way I had been enriched.

All of sudden, in the middle of a sentence, he stopped short and looked me straight in the face. There was a look in his eyes which I cannot forget, a baffled, almost an anxious look; nevertheless he smiled and asked me: 'How do you say "inadequate" in French?' Now this man, by ten or twelve years my senior, is, as I have said, one of France's most honored writers, a man to whom many people look for guidance, the author of several books of permanent value. I laughed and gave him the word, but I did not feel like laughing any more than he felt like smiling. We both understood that this incident, which very few would have even noticed had they witnessed it, carried with it a meaning of importance. I do not wish to dramatize what seems, after all, only a small lapse of memory, but to a man of culture, every word of his mother tongue is a part of a heritage which must be preserved in its entirety, and to forget one of those words is a cause of worry and sadness because it means that something of incalculable worth is being threatened in him.

This is one of the vital problems which a refugee writer has to face. But I have mentioned only one aspect of the question. The counterpart is that our writer has to learn English, not only enough English to carry on the business of everyday life in an English-speaking country, but enough English to express himself as a writer, enough English to do without translators. He existed in former years as a French writer; can he now exist as an English writer? He must lecture. Is he intelligible? He has something to say. Will people over here understand him? Not always. They do not realize what a struggle it is to express one's meaning in a language almost every word of which is a pitfall to foreigners. All they see, all they hear is a man with a tortured face, trying to get the accent on the right syllables and to remember his aitches. And pretty soon they tire of this, and the speaker, if he happens to be the least sensitive, realizes it with distress in his heart and deep humiliation.

But whether they know English or not, there is something which the writers must struggle to preserve: their language. It is the one thing which America will unwittingly take away from them if they do not keep guard over the treasure which their native land has entrusted to their care. They will preserve it, to be sure, by reading books and talking with one another — but if they are alone and if they are too busy to read?

How much is our language really a part of us? In view of the fact that it is possible for us to forget our native tongue, I used to think that languages were superficial, that they didn't go very deep, otherwise how could twelve months' stay in a foreign country make a Frenchman or a German or an Italian hesitate about his prepositions and halt for the most familiar words which he knew as a child? With time I came to revise this opinion. Today I feel pretty sure that our mother tongue gives us something which can never be eradicated.

I have always been interested in this question of languages because of the rather unusual opportunity I was given as a child to learn two languages at the same time. There are so many interesting problems connected with this situation that I may be excused for mentioning my personal case. I was born in Paris of American parents and brought up in that city, much in the manner of most Parisians, that is, I went to one of those large schools called lycées and practically all my friends were French. But at home I was no longer in France, I was in America. My mother's French was a matter of endless mirth to everyone, including herself, and we all spoke English, but I did not speak it well.

To my mother's shame it was a certain time before I could understand English perfectly. As a child I could not bring myself to believe that English was a real language, rather did I take it to be a jumble of meaningless sounds which grown-ups made to pretend they were carrying on a conversation. These sounds I imitated in a spirit of mockery, but years went by before I realized that English words were actually supposed to make sense. I would not understand why, when everything had a name in French, people should go out of their way to call it by some other name. To me the real names of things were French; other names were fancy and unreal. The fact that my father and mother spoke a strange language was simply one of those many things which I vaguely accepted without understanding; it was a part of the mysterious behavior of grown-ups, and as I have mentioned before, I did not believe that in using this strange language they really said anything; I thought they invented these uncouth sounds for the purpose of being funny.

One day something happened which gave me an inkling that the English language was not entirely meaningless. From a psychological point of view the incident is rather curious.

Several times a week my mother read the Bible to us, and she read it in the King James version. I remember that she would sit by a window, book in hand, and my sisters sat around her. I, being very small and not knowing English, was allowed to do as I wished, but I was so fond of my mother that I always sat on the floor at her feet whenever she read to my sisters.

On a certain afternoon as she was reading aloud I amused myself by exploring the cracks in the floor with a pin. It is extraordinary what one could find in those cracks before the days of vacuum cleaners: pins, tiny glass beads which came from goodness knows where, very hard crumbs of bread and, occasionally, a dead insect. All of which was intensely interesting to a child of five. All of a sudden I received something like a shock: I had understood; my mother had read a few words which I understood, they made sense. I got up in great excitement and was made to sit down again. Once more I got up and tugged at my mother's sleeve, but she pushed me gently aside and read on. To this day I can remember how utterly bewildered I felt because I couldn't explain the cause of my excitement.

In later years I made great efforts to call back to memory the first English words I was ever conscious of understanding, but I never succeeded. It is to me a pleasing thought that these words came out of the Bible and I often wonder what they could have been.

I suppose that a novelist would make use of this incident and compare it to the opening of a sluice, with the mighty flow of the English language pouring into the child's brain, but nothing of the kind happened to me. I do not know how I learned English any more than I know how I learned French. The words I had understood that afternoon did not by any means give a key to the whole language, and I was almost as ignorant after hearing them as before, except that I was now conscious of the fact that when my elders spoke in this un-French language they were really saying something. But the biblical words were nothing more from a practical point of view than a streak of lightning in a very black sky.

When a person says that he doesn't know how he learned a language, he means, I think, that it 'came to him naturally.' He understood what was being said in that language before he was even conscious of understanding words. By the time I grasped the meaning of those three or four words from the Bible, a long process had been going on in my brain, probably for several years, and had culminated in the moment which I have described. I had learned without being aware of learning. But as I grew a little older, a book, an English primer, was placed in my hands and I became painfully conscious that I was being taught English.

It was a difficult task. My pronunciation was dreadful and drew deep sighs from my mother who couldn't bear the thought that her son dropped his aitches like a foreigner. Spelling too was the cause of much grief to both of us. This was all the stranger since my sisters learned English with comparative ease; but French was my language, decidedly. Like all children, I was very sensitive, and the idea that when I spoke English I was ridiculous and might be laughed at soon became a sort of fixed idea which hindered my progress in that language.

It is rather odd that such an idea should have persisted in me after any cause for it had disappeared, but I remember that the first year I went to the University I was still so shy of the English language that I had mentally to prepare anything I wanted to say. Even the simplest things like ordering a book from Bruffey's, at the corner, demanded a sort of private rehearsal, and for several months I lived in a state of moral discomfort caused by the possibility of being asked questions in class by my professors and having, as it were, to improvise answers in English. This finally happened and I answered quite well.

For that and other reasons, I am more and more inclined to believe that it is almost an impossibility to be absolutely

bilingual. True, several languages can be mastered by the
same person, sometimes to an amazing degree. I have heard
people turn from French to English and from English to
German with consummate ease and such perfection as to
accent, intonations and choice of words that I wondered if there
wasn't a trick about it. But this is not exactly what I mean.
What I mean is that a man may speak half a dozen languages
fluently and yet feel at home in only one; that is the language in
which he will think when he is alone.

How difficult it is to master completely a language was made
clear to me some years ago in London. I had spent most of the
day with André Gide; we had walked several hours through the
quieter part of the city, discussing books. André Gide is one of
the few persons I know for whom a book is something real and
important, not simply a certain number of pages to be read for
amusement, then tossed aside and dismissed from memory.
What he deems worth reading he reads with admirable care,
always trying to get at the author's intention, which we so
seldom do, and retaining as much of the book as he considers
necessary. The result of such scrupulous reading is, as might be
expected from a mind like his, a stupendous accumulation of
intellectual wealth. Perhaps I should have prefaced my story by
saying that his knowledge of English literature is one which a
scholar might envy. His translation of *Anthony and Cleopatra* and
of the first act of *Hamlet* is considered a definitive piece of work,
and he has done much to introduce such authors as Conrad to
the French reading public.

After we had gone quite a way we both felt tired, and I said I
had to go back to my room. Gide had an appointment in
Chelsea but, not knowing his way round in the maze of London
streets, he asked me to direct him. So I took him to a bus stop
and told him to get off, let us say, at Carlyle Square. 'But,' said
Gide, 'I may not know Carlyle Square when I see it.' 'In that
case,' I replied, 'it might be wiser to ask the conductor to tell
you when you come to it.' 'Of course,' he went on, 'but how

must I tell him?' By that time the bus was in sight, I said: 'All you need to tell him is: Let me off at Carlyle Square.'

'Here,' I thought, as I walked away, 'here is a man who might have carried on a conversation with Andrew Marvell or Henry Vaughan, but cannot address a London bus driver.'

A completely bilingual person is indeed a very rare bird. I have known people who were supposed to speak English as well as French and who, when the effort of speaking in a foreign tongue had been sustained too long, suddenly stumbled over the simplest words. Why this should be I don't quite understand, any more than I can understand why we are not all ambidextrous.

As I have already hinted, my own experience with English was not always a pleasant one. To begin with, I felt so self-conscious when speaking English that I deliberately made those very mistakes which I was striving to avoid; it was as if a sort of perverse imp prompted me to mispronounce certain words, usually when I happened to be speaking to the most fastidious of English writers. That disquieting book, Eighteen Thousand Words Often Mispronounced, would suddenly appear to me in a sort of mental vision and shake its dreadful leaves in my face as I spoke.

I remember that one of the first papers I was asked to write at the university was about Dr. Johnson. The question was as follows: 'Do you consider that Dr. Johnson was a versatile man? If so, prove it.' Now 'versatile' in French means fickle, and little else. The English word, according to the best authorities, may accept this meaning, but more generally signifies many-sided, having many aptitudes. Not being in the least aware of this and having the French word in mind, I wrote what I considered an eloquent vindication of Johnson's moral character. I showed how true he was to Tetty, how consistently kind to his friends, in spite of occasional fits of irritation, and above all how patient and long-suffering he was with Boswell. The paper was read by a young instructor, who returned it to me with a large question mark in blue pencil and the following appreciation: 'Might have been a better paper, had you treated the subject.' So I flew to the Rotunda, looked up 'versatile' in the large edition of Webster, and, in the words of Ethelinda Sapsea's epitaph in *Edwin Drood*, 'with a blush retired.'

In later years I returned to Paris and wrote whatever I had to write in French. It didn't occur to me to do otherwise. I lived in France and the only writing I did in English was in communicating with my friends and relatives in America. But writing letters had little to do with writing books in the same language, or so I thought. This was, I suppose, a French notion; I mean by that, that writing a book, to a Frenchman, is a somewhat more formal process than writing letters. One cannot write a book with the same ease and, alas, the same *désinvolture* as one pens a message to a friend. This is true of any language, but more especially of French, because of the extraordinary importance given to style by French authors. When Buffon put on his best clothes to write in, his most elaborately embroidered coat, his finest lace, he was unwittingly giving us a living symbol of the French attitude towards literature. At times I wonder if such an attitude is not regrettable. It seems to be beyond a doubt that Flaubert's finest writing is to be found not in his novels, great though they be, but in the eight or ten volumes of his letters, many of which were written at top speed with none of those torturing qualms about style which made his literary production so laborious and comparatively so small. It is a rather melancholy thought that, had he devoted less time to worrying over double genitives and words repeated at a distance of only two pages, he might have given us a few more novels of the same quality as *l'Education sentimentale*.

These ideas as to the importance of style still prevail in modern France. A man may be forgiven almost anything he says provided he says it well. On the other hand, a slipshod book has little chance of being permanently accepted. It is an illuminating fact that the boldest of revolutionary French writers between 1920 and 1930 wrote as carefully as the most finicky of poets. Surrealist manifestos of those days were couched in faultless French. They demanded the overthrow of capitalism with an exquisite choice of words. To set fire to the Louvre, that old *idée fixe* of cultured Reds, was advocated in terms of studied ferocity, but grammar and good usage went unscathed through the withering flame of all this eloquence. There is no French writer who at one time or other does not harbor the hope of becoming, so to speak, a part of French tradition. He may be against every kind of tradition in the world if he happens to be a radical, but the tradition of style is still a matter of life and death to a man who wields a pen between the Atlantic Ocean and the Rhine.

Having been brought up in France, I was imbued with these ideas concerning style; some I have kept, and they have become a part of me; others I discarded when I found out that they were more of a hindrance than a help, but they have all taught me something. I considered, as a young man, that one of the great principles of style was to skip all intermediate sentences, according to the rule given by Montesquieu, and I still think it is a good idea. Another principle which I cherished was not to repeat any word on the same page. This may seem a little strange to the English. Indeed it seems strange to me now. When I went back to English to express myself, many of these French notions vanished out of my mind. Words, being like persons in French and in English, had to be treated in a different way in each language.

When I came to this country, in July 1940, I conceived the idea of writing a book about France, not a book on recent events but a book on what I owe to France. I am afraid it would take more than I could write to pay such a debt: nevertheless, I found great pleasure in saying thank you to a nation I love (as I always did), when, having done about ten pages, I had a disquieting thought: 'Who will print these words?' I did not know then that there are French publishers publishing French books in this country. So I laid aside what I had written and decided to begin the book again, this time in English, my intention being to use practically the same words, or, if you wish, to translate my own sentences into English.

At this point something quite unexpected happened. With a very definite idea as to what I wanted to say, I began my book, wrote about a page and a half and, on rereading what I had written, realized that I was writing another book, a book so different in tone from the French that a whole aspect of the subject must of necessity be altered. It was as if, writing in English, I had become another person. I went on. New trains of thoughts were started in my mind, new associations of ideas were formed. There was so little resemblance between what I wrote in English and what I had already written in French that it might almost be doubted that the same person was the author of these two pieces of work. This puzzled me considerably and still does. It hasn't helped me much in understanding the relationship of language to human beings — in a way it has made it seem even more mysterious than I fancied — but it has enabled me to apprehend more clearly the problem of foreign writers who are at present experimenting with the English language.

Translation and the 'Fields of Scripture'

First published in *The American Scholar*,
Vol II, Winter 1941

It is a rather strange fact that for many of us in the English-speaking world, the most important of all books is a translation. The more we think about it the stranger it will seem but we don't think much about it; we just accept it as one of these unalterable facts, like the shape of America, for instance. And yet it is in itself a very remarkable fact. India has her sacred books, so have Persia and Japan, and those books are their own. Our sacred books, which we call the Bible, are borrowed books; they did not primarily belong to us, yet they do now through that very delicate and complicated process called translation.

When people quote the Bible in English-speaking countries they usually quote the King James Version, still the most widely-read version in spite of repeated and not wholly unjustified attempts to dethrone it. For millions of readers it is a hallowed translation, but it is interesting to note that we don't call it a translation; we call it a version. We do not speak of a version of Marcel Proust or a version of Montaigne or even of a version of Dante; but we do speak of the Greek Version, of the Douay Version, of the King James Version of the Bible. This in itself is significant. Translation and version are close kin, so far as meaning is concerned, but their connotations differ. Translation is given the preference in modern speech and may be applied to thousands of writings, good or bad, but version is different, version is almost venerable.

A version is literally the act of turning or changing. A book is turned or changed into something else but in the case of the Bible there is, as regards the King James Version, a vague and inexpressed feeling that the original has, so to speak, changed itself into itself. The reason is that this translation of the Bible is so closely connected with the thought and feeling of the English race that it has become a part of it; it is the book even of those who do not read it but whose heritage it nevertheless constitutes. At the time when the Revised Version was being intro-

duced in this country and met with the opposition of so many
people, a pious man in a less enlightened part of the United
States was reported to have said that, so far as he was concerned, he would never read the Revised Version, adding, with
great indignation, that the Lord's words were not to be
tampered with: they stood in the Bible exactly as He had
spoken them and it was inconceivable that anyone should dare
to alter them. It became clear, upon questioning the man, that
he believed the Lord to have addressed Israel in English. Now,
from the strict point of view of exegesis he was laboring under a
delusion but there was something very moving and very real in
what he said; the race to which he belonged spoke through his
lips.

Throughout the centuries the Jews have called themselves
the People of the Book. The Anglo-Saxon race has an equal
claim to this proud and beautiful title. Even, and I should say
particularly when Anglo-Saxons revolt against it, they still
belong to the Book. It is theirs and they are its own. I do not
mean that it is theirs exclusively — it belongs to the whole
world — but it has stamped them in a very definite way and
made them what they are. When Samuel Butler took his Bible
and flung it into a corner he was making an intensely Anglo-
Saxon gesture. He rejected the Bible violently and in doing so
admitted the power of the Book over him. Had he been Italian,
for instance, he would never have flung his Bible in a corner for
the simple reason that in all probability he would not have
owned one.

Most Anglo-Saxons, then, when reading their Bible are not
conscious of reading a translation. They love it as sincerely as
the Jew loves the Hebrew original, and in a certain sense we
may say that it is love that naturalized the Hebrew Bible and
made it an English book. They feel that in a way the translation
is an original in itself; that the book was rewritten in English
rather than translated; they believe that the spirit of the

Hebrew Bible has found its way into the English Bible.* But of course the fact remains that the English Bible is a translation and if we compare it diligently, not with former translations but with the original, we shall discover that it is sometimes strangely inaccurate.

Like a great many American children I was brought up on the King James Version. My mother read it to us and she read it well, not in ministerial tones, she could not have done that, but reverently and yet naturally. She handed me the book as it had been handed to her — that is, she taught me to love it, and that love has endured; but when I was about sixteen I discovered two other versions which I read with unequal pleasure. One was a French version, the other was the Vulgate.

The French version[9] was very learned, with explanatory notes at the bottom of each page. At first I did not care for it very much. It seemed to me that this was not the Bible, but I could not exactly understand why. What I considered so beautiful in the English version sounded a little flat in French and, I hesitate to use the word, a little dull. I was puzzled and disappointed.

From the Vulgate I received a very different impression. To begin with, owing to my ignorance and ingenuousness, I thought that, Latin being older than either English or French, the Vulgate must of necessity be nearer to the original. Quite apart from that, I was awed by the magnificence of the language as well as by the venerable age of the translation. This, I said to myself, is the Bible the Christian Church was reading when England was still peopled with illiterate half-savages who could barely express anything like a thought. Each sentence seemed bathed in incense. The most familiar and simplest phrases of the English Bible appeared here clothed in a majesty the like of which I had never dreamed. It was a real joy

---

* In referring to the English Bible I mean the King James Version. The Catholic or Douay Version is not discussed here because it was not made directly from the original tongues.

to read the Prophets in this superb language which, as it were, had 'caught their shrieks in cups of gold.' I did not dare entertain the thought that this book was not the Bible; indeed I might rather have been tempted to believe that it was the Bible, to the exclusion of any other version. At any rate it was not, in my mind, the same book as the King James Version; it belonged to a different world and seemed permeated with a different spirit.

I found myself in the position of a man who is presented with several portraits, allegedly portraits of the same person, and who cannot see a satisfactory likeness between them. I took it for granted that these portraits, so different in style and in spirit, were portraits of the same person because I had been told that they were and I had no means of investigating the matter. But I was not content with what I had been told though it did not yet enter my mind to controvert any part of this teaching. I assented unwillingly.

As years went by I familiarized myself sufficiently with the German language to read Luther's Version with some appreciation of its literary beauty. A new aspect of the old problem confronted me here. In many respects I found this version very similar in spirit to the King James Version. They were obviously portraits of the same person. So I was led to believe that they offered a better likeness of the original than the other translations I had examined. This was natural enough, I suppose, although I grant that my methods were anything but scientific. I must add that, in speaking of the likeness of a translation to the original, I am referring for the present moment only to a similarity in spirit or, if you prefer, to a similarity in the impressions conveyed by the two books. This similarity of spirit was not at all remarkable or fortuitous, considering how closely connected German is with English.

However, on examining certain parts of these two translations I discovered something which struck me as rather peculiar: they did not always exactly agree. For example the fourth verse in the well-known 23rd psalm reads in English, as you remember, 'Yea, though I walk through the valley of the shadow of death, I will fear no evil' etc. Whereas in German we have, '*Und ob ich schon wanderte im finstern Tal, fürchte ich kein Unglück.*' Where was the shadow of death? Feeling a little mystified I opened the Vulgate and read, '*Nam et si ambulavero in medio umbrae mortis, non timebo mala.*' What had become of the valley? The German version kept the valley and did away with the shadow of death. Saint Jerome gave us the shadow of death but deprived us of the valley. The English gave us both, and for that matter so did the French, but why didn't the Latin and the German?

Of course the meaning of the verse was substantially the same in the four translations. But turning over the leaves of the English Bible I came to psalm 84 for which I had always had a particular fondness, 'How amiable are thy tabernacles ...' Verses 5 and 6 of this psalm read as follows in the King James Version: 'Blessed is the man whose strength is in Thee; in whose heart are the ways of them. [Here I paused, as I always did, wondering if I quite understood what I was reading, but I went on.] Who passing through the valley of Baca make it a well; the rain also filleth the pools.' This was very obscure; neither did the marginal notes help me much by telling me that the valley of Baca was the valley of mulberry trees. So I opened the Vulgate and this is what I found: '*Beatus vir, cujus est auxilium abs te: ascensiones in corde suo disposuit, in valle lacrimarum, in loco quem posuit.*'

I rubbed my eyes. The rain-filled pools had disappeared like a mirage. I made sure that I was reading the same psalm, picked up the German Bible and in the corresponding place read as follows: '*Wohl den Menschen, die dich für ihre Stärke halten und von Herzen dich nachwandeln, die durch das Jammertal gehen und machen daselbst Brunnen; und die Lehrer werden mit viel Segen geschmückt.*' So the pools were there after all and with them,

astoundingly enough, teachers. My investigations ended there
for the moment and I closed the book with a feeling of uneasiness and also a feeling of distrust which I could not quite
conquer.

In one of the most famous books written by Jewish mystics,
the *Zohar*, there is a very remarkable passage on the Bible. As I
remember it the Bible is compared to a large and mighty
fortress. People walk around the high walls and look up at the
battlements but that is about all they see of that fortress. Inside
the stronghold, however, there is a very beautiful girl. She is a
prisoner and tries to communicate with her lover who is
outside. He looks and looks at the walls and suddenly, through
a crack between two stones, the girl's hand is seen waving to
him. The girl, of course, is the spirit or hidden meaning of the
book; her lover is the Bible student who is in love with the holy
word.

I too felt that I was standing in front of a fortress when I read
translations of the Bible and the prisoner in that fortress was
the Hebrew language which could only peer, as it were,
through the cracks in the somber walls and make signs to the
lover of the book.

In 1919 I attended the University of Virginia. It was there, at
a bookstore, that I had my first glance at a Hebrew Bible, which
I immediately bought with a grammar to accompany it. I could
not get back to my room fast enough to start on the alphabet but
my troubles began there and then. I had to ask a Jewish student
how to pronounce the consonants and he hinted broadly that
since I wasn't a Jew I could never do this successfully. When he
revealed to me that I should have to master no less than seven
conjugations I was appalled. I suggested that he read me the
very first verse in Genesis. He did, with infinite solemnity. It
seemed to come from the very beginning of creation; now soft,
now raucous, the strange syllables carried one back through an
almost unthinkable space of time, back and back through the
centuries to the days when man first addressed himself to the

Almighty, using, I fancied then, these very sounds to express his thought.

The very antiquity of Hebrew had something dreadful about it. So did the grammar. I had somewhat taken heart when I heard my Jewish friend read the opening words of Genesis but my enthusiasm waned considerably when, upon being left alone, I opened the Hebrew grammar and came up against the rules of accentuation. Very soon I closed the book and put it away with the Hebrew Bible in an honorable place, on the top shelf of my bookcase. The fortress looked grimmer than ever.

My interest in Hebrew revived suddenly ten years later after much time spent in floundering among contradictory versions of the Bible. But now I was determined to arrive at some kind of result. So I consulted a friend of mine at the Collège de France (I was then living in Paris). He advised me to ask a rabbi to teach me Hebrew, adding that rabbis were the only people who really knew that language.

It was not very difficult to find a rabbi in Paris in 1935. I doubt that mine knew anything but the Old Testament but that he knew from cover to cover, by heart and in the original tongue. This knowledge I envied him more than words can express. He produced a typewritten grammar of his own which I immediately proceeded to learn by heart and on the second day we plunged forthwith into the first chapter of Isaiah. This too I learned by heart. Page after page of the Bible was committed to memory in true Oriental fashion. Never had I made such an effort in my whole life but I was amply repaid. After many months of obstinate work I acquired a slight knowledge of Hebrew and thus I was able to catch a glimpse of the face I had known heretofore only through the medium of portraits.

Now at last I could walk through what the *Imitation of Christ* so beautifully calls the fields of Scripture, *prata Scripturarum*, nor did I any longer have to depend on a translator to find my way about; I ventured to run away from my guide, for a few steps at

first, then for long rambles during which I more than once fell
into ditches or got lost in what commentators call *loci desperati*,
but I knew enough to realize that I was wandering in a land the
beauty of which I had only faintly suspected; it was one of the
oldest countries in the world but to me it seemed as new as
though the weary armies of translators had never set foot in it.
The 23rd psalm was not simply a series of fairsounding words
to be chanted in a church; it was an oasis like those I had seen
on the skirts of the African desert, with the shade of date-palms
darkening the waters of rest. And when the wind arose, as it so
often does in the Old Testament, it was not simply 'an horrible
tempest'; it was something sinister that screeched and howled
through the guttural Hebrew consonants. When David raged
against his enemies he did not do so in the exalted style of an
English divine of the 17th century; he was more like a wild-eyed
desert chief, with rasping sounds coming from his throat, and
frantic gesticulation.

All this of course was only a first impression but it was a very
powerful one. I sensed that it was what translators cannot
translate, try as they may, learned and sincere though they
be; however diligently they may compare the result of their
efforts with the original, the Hebraic quality of the book cannot
pass from one language into another; to be sure the spirit is
there — Israel knew how to speak to the whole world — but
something is lost which can be retrieved only by going back to
the source.

It was an exciting experience, this working my way back to
the original of a book I had always so deeply admired, but I was
imperfectly equipped for the task; my knowledge of Hebrew
was very scanty, and I can never hope to acquire the feeling for
that language that a man of Jewish blood might possess.
Nevertheless it taught me much about the difficulties of translating. I remember that one day when I had finished reading a
difficult passage in Isaiah with my professor, I asked him if he
considered that a good translation could be given of these

verses. He instantly said no. I asked him why. 'It is a poem,' he answered, a little evasively.

This in itself might appear a sufficient reason to many, but there are other difficulties. As I have said before, since translations sometimes differ to an amazing degree it is a thankless task to try to get at the correct meaning of a Scripture text by comparing one translation with another. This verse may yield a more satisfactory meaning in the French translation whereas the following may sound more logical in the English, and so forth from Genesis to Malachi. Is there such a thing as a perfect translation of the Bible? That admirable feat of scholarship, the Revised Version, often shows signs of bewilderment in the face of mangled or corrupt readings.

Some books of the Bible have fared better than others in their long journey through the centuries. In spite of serious gaps the historical books as a whole afford a good and consistent meaning; but many chapters in the Book of Job, for instance, have come down to us in such a state of mutilation that the work of translators is reduced almost to guesswork. One of the most authoritative works on the subject, the translation and commentary of Father Dhorme, offers an extraordinary picture of what might be called the battle of translators. Biblical students of every creed and language are profusely quoted, some verses allowing as many as twenty different interpretations. In many cases only three or four tantalizing words remain where we should need a dozen to make a satisfactory meaning. How much would be left of our own books had they undergone such disfigurement? There is a very beautiful poem by Victor Hugo about a beggar whom the author takes into his house and feeds. The beggar is cold and weary and the cloak around his shoulders is drenched with rain. So the poet gives him a bowl of milk, makes him sit down, and, taking his cloak from him, holds it up to the fire to dry it. The cloak has a great many holes in it and as it is held up in front of the fire the glow of the flames shines through the holes like stars in a black sky. The Book of

Job is like that beggar's cloak: it is torn to shreds but through the rents in the texture one can see the stars gleaming.

I realize that the difficulty I have mentioned is more directly connected with criticism than with translation proper, but the trouble with some of our older and venerable versions is that they did not always have sound criticism to back them. When they felt uncertain they gave us a paraphrase. Now this raises a question of enormous interest to translators at large: in cases where a literal translation would not 'sound well' isn't it justifiable to use a paraphrase — that is, to substitute for certain words others which are not exact equivalents but do convey the same general meaning?

In Hebrew, as in all languages, there are words and phrases that cannot possibly be translated literally because they would lose much of their meaning in the process. For example, one does not say in Hebrew that a man is forty or fifty; one says that he is the son of forty or fifty years. From a philosophical point of view I am sure this goes very far. In the same way a person guilty of a capital crime is called the son of death. The translators of the English Bible, when confronted with expressions such as these, did their best to render them into English as literally as possible. They were so penetrated with the value of each word in the Scriptures that they preferred to run the risk of making English wear Hebrew garments, as it were, rather than force the language of the Scriptures to dress up as English, lest English betray the spirit of the original. Perhaps I can best explain what I mean by drawing attention to what was happening to the Bible in 17th-century France. A translation was being made there also but the approach was different. Here, thought your French translator, is an Oriental book which I shall try to turn into a French book in order that the French reader may understand it. The principle he went on seemed sound enough in those days — it would have been sound for any book except the Bible. As a result, in some passages where the English Bible uses the good old word *belly*, the corresponding word in the French Bible is *heart* because heart is more polite.

It is interesting to see how modern the English translators were in their attitude towards translating. They were determined to give England a Hebrew book and, within certain limits, they succeeded; they succeeded because — and this is the point I want to stress — they understood that in the case of such a book as the Bible only a literal translation will do. This is all the more striking since they lived at a time when foreign books were translated with anything but literal accuracy, in English or in any other tongue. A fascinating study could be made of Hebrew phrases that have crept into the English language and have become a part of it through the English Bible.*

But the real problem of translating a book goes far beyond coining happy phrases and giving us smooth-reading sentences; it is that of catching the spirit of the language from which the translation is made. Ernest Renan used to say that Hebrew is a child's language. Indeed, it has the limitations and the virtues of a primitive language; its vocabulary is very small compared with the vocabulary of classical Greek, for instance, and its syntax allows little variety in expressing thoughts or telling a story. Moreover, it is curiously deficient in some of its parts and almost superabundant in others. Its very elements seem contradictory. To a certain coarseness of texture it allies an exquisite variety of tones; it is like a rich and delicate embroidery on rough material. A modern philosopher would feel very much hampered were this language his only means of exposing his views; it is significant that later Jewish philosophers of the pre-Christian era resorted to Greek to express themselves. Yet it is most interesting that the book which tells

---

* One expression I strongly suspect of being Hebrew in origin rather than purely English is 'to set one's heart upon something,' for this is literally and word for word what the Hebrew says to express the same thought. 'High-handed' might likewise be traced back to a Hebrew origin.

us of the invisible world in terms of unsurpassed magnificence should be written in a language so closely bound to the world of the senses.

Some languages offer a better medium than others to the translator of the Hebrew Scriptures. French cannot be considered very propitious because French, like Latin — and French, as Remy de Gourmont said, is Latin ('*le latin continué*') — tends towards the abstract; English I suppose will undergo the same process in time but in English as we know it, a more primitive element, almost lacking in French, has been preserved. French could never furnish us with such an emotionally disturbing word as *doom*; it would say 'final judgment,' with a direct appeal to the intellect. *Jugement dernier* makes me think, whereas the Crack of Doom makes me feel like running for shelter under a mountain. And there lies the difference.

In preference to the more intellectual beauty of Latinistic words the barbaric beauty of many Anglo-Saxon words is invaluable to the translator of the Bible. There is also a rhythm in the English language that is akin to the rhythm of Hebrew poetry — that rhythm which has so felicitously been compared with 'the rapid stroke as of alternate wings, the heaving and sinking of the troubled heart.' In the words of Tyndale, 'The properties of the Hebrew tongue agree a thousand times more with the English than with the Latin. The manner of speaking is both one, so that in a thousand places thou needest but to translate it into English, word for word.'

It would therefore seem desirable that the translator of the Bible consider himself the slave of the Book, repeating, if possible, word for word what his master tells him. The Bible has not fared well at the hands of writers who were too conscious of their art. From the point of view of French, Renan's translation of the Book of Job is an admirable piece of work in that simple, easy, slightly oily style which subsequent writers tried hard to imitate. But is it the Book of Job in its stark majesty? I rather think that it gives us, instead of Job, a picture of Ernest Renan seated in his frockcoat among the ashes. So far as the translation of the Bible is concerned, no art at all is consummate art. Every ten years or so, or more frequently, new versions of the Bible are produced in one language or the other. This is a sign of the enormous vitality of the book and of the difficulties that confront its interpreters. Translations become old-fashioned and it sometimes happens that the very language in which they are written ages and dies. But Scripture remains ever young, ever fresh, with a perpetual challenge to the art of translating.

My First Book in English

Written in 1941, Julian Green refers in this essay to his book, *Memories of Happy Days*, his first to be entirely written in English.

Until 1940 I wrote all my books in French. I wrote them in French because I was born in Paris, and was brought up in Paris, and lived in Paris. When I had anything to say, I instinctively had recourse to French. French is the language in which I learned almost everything I know. When I was a child and heard people speaking in a foreign tongue, I wondered what madness drove them to make those strange sounds when there were so many French words at their disposal. French words, in my mind, were the only possible designation of all we see around us as well as all that goes on inside our brain. Foreign words belonged to the realm of fancy. They could be written and pronounced this way, or, conceivably, written and pronounced this other way, and it didn't really matter, whereas a French word could only be exactly what it was, as it was. I could not imagine that there should ever have been a time when the sky had not been called *le ciel*, or that there should ever be a time when it would no longer be called *le ciel*.

What bothered me more than I can say was that my mother spoke to me in English, and I had great trouble in learning that language. Only a philosopher could explain what the English language did to me. I felt that in teaching me these new words, my mother was trying to make a sort of duplicate of the universe, which, I thought, was a French universe.

It took me years of hard work to finally enter into what might be called the universe of the English tongue and to appreciate its poetic quality. A language is not only a means of expressing oneself, it is also, it is particularly, a mode of seeing and of feeling. Each race reconstructs the universe according to its own ideas. An English word does not limit itself to the designation of such and such an object, or such and such a natural phenomenon; it renders, in its own particular way, the impression created in an English mind by that object or that natural phenomenon. Going a little further, one might even say that a language is a sort of human commentary on creation.

The mystery of words is one of the most fascinating in the world. How many among us, in our childhood, have painstakingly repeated certain words the sound of which fell strangely on our ear, and because it fell so strangely, we never tired of hearing it, as if some kind of magic had been connected with it. I remember that, when I was extremely young, I was fascinated by the name of Paris. I wondered why my native city was called by that name and not by another. And the more I repeated that name, the more extraordinary it seemed to me. I thought that by saying it to myself over and over again a sufficient number of times, I might finally discover something about it, although what I thought I might discover, I cannot say; but I never discovered anything, except that Paris was called Paris.

My own name would also cause me to lose myself in endless reveries. I found it extremely curious that a certain combination of sounds should designate me in such a way that, by making those sounds, one could reasonably expect to see me appear. I hope not to sound too childish if I say that to this day the designation of objects and beings has lost nothing of its old fascination for me. The source of much poetry lies right there. Almost all children are poets, that is, they often have a sense of the mystery of creation. They are in this world like strangers who have just arrived in an unknown country, and they look around with much surprise. Now, one of the aims of education is to do away by degrees with the feeling of surprise, by explaining to the child the meaning of what puzzles him. And, growing up, he feels more and more at home in a world where little is left that can surprise him any more. Thus do poets give up the ghost. The poet is a man who retains in himself what might be called a sense of mystery and the ability to experience surprise. We have all been poets at a time which we can hardly remember. Whenever an aspect of the sky, or of the earth, or of the sea strikes a note of pleasant sadness in us and causes us to be silent, we may be sure that the poet is not quite dead.

Is one the same person in French as in English? I mean, does one say the same things? Does one think in the same way in both languages and in terms which are, so to speak, interchangeable? I do not pretend to be able to solve such difficult problems, but it might be interesting to examine them. Sometimes I am tempted to think that the roots of the human language go very deep in our personality. To teach a child a language in preference to another is to interfere with that child's manner of being for the rest of his days. A little Frenchman does not see the universe as does a little American, and that is due, for the most part, to the language through which the universe is, so to speak, presented to them. After all, we are what we think. If we are taught to think French thoughts, it seems inevitable that sooner or later we shall be French, because a language is, first and foremost, a mode of thought.

However, there are other times when I feel inclined to believe quite the opposite of what I have just written. Perhaps, after all, these problems of expression are only superficial. I have noticed that a great many foreigners who settle in America end by forgetting what is considered the good usage in their mother tongue, unless they struggle to defend that portion of their national heritage. After a certain time, traces of foreign infiltration can be discerned in their speech. I do not mean that foreign words are boldly substituted for French words, or for Spanish or German words, such as the case may be, but that French, or Spanish, or German words are used with a meaning which they could have only in English.

Canadian French is full of such words or phrases. Quite recently I was looking at a little prayer book printed in Canada, and at the bottom of several pages I read these words: 'Tournez à la page 15,' or 'tournez à la page 72,' which is, of course, a literal translation from the English, but can hardly be called French, yet all the words are French. What we have here is really English dressed up as French. There are, unfortunately, innumerable examples of that strange language which is neither French nor English. I have heard French people in America speak of So-and-So having registered for military duty and using the word *enregistrer*, which is used in France for luggage.

Those are the weakest points in the language's line of defense. The last retrenchments are taken when words in one language are simply substituted for words in another. Sometimes a man who is living in a foreign country will make up words, which his native language cannot supply him with. I remember reading an article in a French paper printed in this country and coming across a word which I had never seen: *inconquérable*, a literal translation of the English 'unconquerable'. *Inconquérable* does not exist in French, the only word that can take its place being *invincible*, yet no one with a good knowledge of French will deny that invincible does not completely render the meaning of 'unconquerable'.

Although I can no longer dwell on this particular linguistic problem, I should like to say a word about one of the many difficulties I encountered as I was translating some poems by Charles Péguy. One day I was confronted with the word *sainte*. A simple word, easy enough to translate, you might think. Doesn't a saint mean *une sainte*? Oh, yes. But suppose, as was the case, you had to translate: *saints et saintes*. I thought and thought, I racked my brain, but it has never been my good luck to find an English word to designate a woman who has been canonized for the same reason. You can't very well use the expression 'holy woman', because holy women are not necessarily saints, far from it.

It is possible to forget one's native tongue. Does that mean that the roots of a language do not reach as far as we should like to think? I can only ask the question.

In former years, I believe that I should have tried to come to some kind of conclusion, but today it seems to me that conclusions which are reached by sheer willpower are seldom satisfactory and of much less interest than the questions which they purpose to solve. Uncertainty seems to be somehow nearer truth, in many cases, than categorical answers.

Be that as it may, I am not now trying to establish laws; I simply wish to tell what my observations have been in a certain field of language. In July 1940 I had the idea of writing a book on France as I knew her in my childhood and the early part of my youth. In the preface to the book, I have explained all the reasons which prompted me to undertake that task, a task which I considered a duty. My intention was no more than to tell the story of my life.

I began my book in French, of course, and I say 'of course' because up to that time I had practically never written in any other language than French. The first pages were written with relative ease. To write about oneself is never an impossible task, and we are all of us justified in believing that our childhood memories are as interesting as other people's. Art consists in presenting them in the most acceptable way. That is why I speak of the task as being easy, but only relatively so. For I must confess that I have never found it easy to write down words on a piece of paper in such a way that they will hold the reader's attention.

I wrote about twenty pages. At this point I put down my pen and wondered who was going to print my book and who was going to read it. You must remember that in July 1940 French publishers in the States were very few in number. Personally, I didn't know one. As for the readers of French books, there were some, to be sure, but terribly scattered. Would it not be more natural, in an English-speaking country, to write this book in English? All the more since my book, the object of which was to serve France, was principally meant for American readers.

For all those reasons, I decided to put aside the pages I had already written in French and to make a completely new start, in English. This was, for me, something of an adventure. I had, of course, written a large number of letters in English, I had even written a short story in that language, but never a book.* However, I set myself to work. I approached the English language as you might approach a person you know quite well and who, nevertheless, intimidates you, a little. That was because, in many ways, the English language is a very formidable person. Voltaire, speaking of the French language, called it a proud hussy. I don't know that anybody would dare call English such names, but I remember that when I wrote the first sentence in my book, I felt extremely uncertain.

The best I could do, it seemed to me, was to use the very simplest words I could muster, the everyday words which my mother taught me as a child, and I really believe that I succeeded in saying what I wanted to say. There were several reasons for that. First, what I had to say was in no wise very complicated: all I purposed to do was to tell the story of a small boy who had been brought up at Passy. Also I was convinced and still am, for that matter, that the plainest vocabulary is almost always sufficient to express even the subtlest of ideas. It was therefore quite unnecessary to put on airs, as the saying goes.

Having written about two dozen pages, I summoned my courage and read what I had written. What struck me most,

---

'The Apprentice Psychiatrist,' first written as a term paper for an English class at the University of Virginia. It is reprinted here starting on page 235.

however, was how little these English sentences resembled the French sentences I had written on the same subject. Now, what I expected to read was a sort of unconscious translation from the French, or at least a very close equivalent, whereas what I saw might have been written by another hand than mine.

I don't want to imply more than I mean. The subject was the same. The choice of details quite different. I did not say the same things in both languages, because, when writing in English, I had the feeling that in some obscure way I was not quite the same person. I realize that this must sound a little strange and I shall not try to draw any conclusions. All I wish to do is to state a fact as clearly as possible.

There is an Anglo-Saxon way of approaching a subject, just as there is a French way. The difference between the two is essential, although not easily defined. Also, the choice of words — I was about to say the choice of colors — varies considerably from one language to another. It has sometimes been denied, but I nevertheless think it true, that ideas are unconsciously suggested to us by words. John Keats once said that his thoughts were guided by words, and the same could be said of a number of great poets. I am convinced that words can cause a book to completely deviate from its course, unless the author's ear be perfectly attuned to the subtle music of language. There are certain registers of thought which can be touched upon by the French language with greater felicity than by other languages, just as there are thoughts which seem to be provoked and brought to fullness and maturity more readily by English. My quarrel with translators is that they take that delicate instrument called the French or the English language and that they use it to play out of tune, out of time, and off the key. Have you never had a feeling of mental discomfort in reading a translation, and don't you agree with me that such a feeling of discomfort is analogous to the distress caused by a musical instrument pitched either too high or too low? Take the best possible translations. Take, for instance, Mallarmé's translation of 'Ulalume', or Francis Thompson's 'Heard on the Mountain', which is a translation of Hugo's *'Ce qu'on entend sur la montagne'*. Our pleasure in reading those translations may be very keen, but it is not unmixed with a certain vague feeling of irritation, a sort of impatience due to the fact that behind the veil of French and English words breathes a thought that is foreign to the language in which it is expressed. There is a perpetual disagreement between the words and what the words are struggling to say, a discord not without a charm of its own, one might almost say a dissonance; now, we all know how pleasing a dissonance can be to a musically trained ear, and I am sure we have all come across the person who thinks that Edgar Allan Poe's writings are insufferable except in Baudelaire's rendering of them.

In speaking of translations, I seem to have gone from the path I was following a while ago, but the problem that confronted me when I wrote my first book in English had many points in common with the translator's. The difference between a good and a bad translator is that the bad translator thinks in the language from which he is translating, whereas the good translator thinks in the language of his translation. My ambition was to be the good translator of a book I had not written, if I may say, a book which I might have written in French, and hadn't, a book which I wanted to think in English. It is not for me to say whether I have failed or succeeded in my attempt, if I have caught that interior rhythm of English which is so different from the general gait of French. But I do know that, when I read the proofs of my book, some months later, I was very much surprised: I understood perfectly the state of mind of a hen who rises from her brood and sees a duckling walk away from under her wing.

This brings me to a very delicate problem, I mean the influence exerted by a language on the person who uses it. To speak a language is to lend oneself to the influence of that language, and indeed to the influence of a whole race. The

Anglo-Saxon race is characterized by an extreme reticence in expressing its feelings. This reticence, often mistaken for coldness, is the cause of many erroneous impressions, but I do not think anything can be done about it, any more than about the leopard's spots. What one might call effusiveness is not a very frequent phenomenon in English literature, except in poetry, but English poetry is really the safety valve which prevents the machine from bursting. A Frenchman, as a rule, has far fewer inhibitions and hesitates very little to express what he feels. Hence a literature very different in character, and a poetry which seldom has the same compensatory value.

In reading the proofs of my book, I was struck by all that I had left unsaid and that I should most certainly have said in that book, had I written it in French. For instance, all that had to do with the development of religious feeling. I was even tempted to suppress the little I had said on that subject in the second half of the book. Why? I cannot say. Probably because I had written the book in English. It was as if the language itself had opposed certain disclosures in a book of that type. Had I been willing to give the book a more serious turn, it might have been possible to enlarge on spiritual problems, but I didn't want the book to be too serious.

In French it is much easier to pass from a serious to a lighter vein. The language itself seems to wear a smile, and yet, without ceasing to smile, it knows how to be as grave as possible. That is what makes a French style, and a French mind, so very difficult to analyze. In English, somehow, one is always keenly aware of coming very close to indiscretion, whereas French manages to cross the border and be safely back home without arousing too much attention.

Imparting one's secret in English almost always involves a certain amount of moral discomfort. There is a French expression which I have always found very apt: *se livrer*, that is, to confide, to impart some personal matter. *Littré* tells us that *se livrer* simply means 'to be communicative.' But if we look at the word closely, what does it really mean? It means to give up one's freedom, just as a man delivers himself into the hands of an adversary. Of course, that is not what is meant in ordinary conversation, not quite that, and yet he who is ready to impart some secret personal matter will sooner or later find himself in a state of inferiority, unless his confidence is repaid in kind. He will be at a disadvantage. If, however, his interlocutor is generous and well-bred, he will in his turn mention confidential matters so as not to retain an unfair advantage. All of which has somewhat to do with strategy. But our social life is of such a cast that we all of us live more or less behind barricades which we have built at great pains with our own hands. To learn how to build those barricades is a part of our education. From one barricade to another, we parley, but we do not give in, we do not deliver ourselves into the hands of our adversary: that would be disgraceful. Sometimes, however, it happens that some of us get bored behind our barricades; we feel lonely: so we pull out our handkerchiefs which we use as white flags to ask for a truce.

Well, a Frenchman is willing enough to come down from his invisible barricade. There are even instances of his breaking his barricade to pieces, like Jean-Jacques Rousseau, who in consequence experienced endless misfortunes. But your Englishman entrenches himself behind a barricade which resembles a system of fortifications, and such a complicated system of fortifications that the Englishman himself is somewhat at a loss to know how to get out of it. He is willing to take a few steps forward, he does so, not ungraciously, but one can't help feeling that he addresses his fellow men from afar, from the slope of a glacis. He is extremely guarded in everything he says, he does not expose himself by unwise confidences. This attitude is common to the whole race, and certainly quite justifiable. We might call it a spirit of courteous defense. At any rate, it seems to have pervaded the language itself, and that, I suppose, is why a confidence is more difficult to make in English than in

French, to say nothing of a confession. An Englishman is always afraid of hearing more than he should, of being told a secret which he does not wish to share. Why? Because it might force him into a kind of reciprocity of confidence, for which he has a particular loathing, and should he refuse to requite confidence with confidence, an embarrassing situation might follow: that, too, he wishes to avoid. Hence a reserve which is nothing more than the desire to defend his freedom and privacy; a reserve which has become instinctive. Language, as we all know, reflects what is most deeply instinctive in a race, and that is probably why, when an Englishman struggles free from his usual reserve and delivers himself of uncalled-for confidences, the hearer is often made to feel uncomfortable, as I have said. English is a very direct and positive language, and unless a man uses it with all the necessary skill, he may find himself saying far more than he intended.

You can now understand why I felt a little uncertain as I wrote the opening pages of my first book in English. I found it above all difficult to realize what impression my words, my English words, would make on the reader, but I enjoyed the adventure of writing in English: it took me back to the time when I wrote my first book in French, when words still seemed new to the inexperienced writer.

So far, I have said nothing of one of my main difficulties in writing my book, the first book of mine that was not a novel; I might, of course, call it a novel, but it was a novel written by life and transcribed by me. A few observations on the novel may not here be out of place. We all know that the novelist borrows from life everything he needs to write his novels. But there are many ways of borrowing from life. Some novelists believe that the observations they make in everyday life can very well be used in novels. What is true in real life is necessarily true in a novel, because a novel is a reflection of life. Such a theory must seem extremely sensible. It has produced a great number of novels written on the assumption that that elusive thing called

life can be caught and imprisoned in a book. I do not say that
the theory is right or wrong. Such theories as that are right or
wrong inasmuch as the books to which they give birth are good
or bad. But I do believe that, when the books are bad, it is
because their authors have labored under a delusion: they
believed that by copying life with slavish accuracy, a writer is
able to reproduce it, to grasp it, as it were, in its very essence.
Unfortunately, it is not so easy as that. An imitation of life is a
dead thing. The problem is not to copy, but to create anew.
Nothing is quite so motionless as a photograph album. It is
useless to tell me that a photograph does not lie, that it is an
indisputable likeness of life itself; I can see no more in a
photograph than the reflection of an absent person. And many
of the novels we read are nothing but photograph albums.

Now, life is the greatest of all novelists, and an inimitable
one. But it is not possible to take that novelist's books and copy
them. What is remarkable about life is that, as far as writing
novels is concerned, it never furnishes us with anything ready-
made. An incident taken from real life may seem absolutely
false if it is put in a book without the necessary adjustments.
This, in my mind, has never been sufficiently observed and will
always puzzle me somewhat, because it does not seem logical.
One would be tempted to believe that what is true in life is true
anywhere, or at any rate should be true in a novel which
purports to give a picture of life. We know, however, that it is
not so. Nothing can be quite so lifeless as certain novels of the
eighties and nineties, which were nevertheless written with an
almost fanatical regard for accuracy. Notes and observations,
be they ever so meticulous, cannot alone put life in a novel.
Here we come up against a law which is apparently without
exception. In order to write a novel with a reasonable chance of
surviving at least one generation of readers, it is indispensable
to have what we might call a sense of life, and no amount of
notes and observations can possibly help us if we haven't.

I do not mean that observation is unnecessary. On the

contrary, we cannot do without it, but it remains nevertheless true that Balzac was never more faithful to life than when he invented his characters and what they had to say. Indeed, it was by inventing that he recreated life. Observation and memory are the two sources of the novelist's invention, but it is neither observing nor remembering that creates a kinship between life and the novelist, it is inventing. Life is continually inventing. To be sure, from time to time life, the oldest of all novelists, is somewhat repetitious — I suppose from overwork — but we cannot create the same effects as life by merely copying the works of that famous author, we must invent, just as life does, with the greatest possible freedom. We need not fear to be overbold, if we retain a sense of reality. How tame the most daring of our inventions compared with what life makes up every day! I am always amazed at critics who read novels and when something strikes them as being a little out of the ordinary, exclaim that the incident is not true to life. Don't they ever read the papers? Newspapers, incoherent and ill written though they be, are nevertheless pages from a first-rate novel. Life has never been afraid of writing an unlikely novel; life cares very little about the opinions of critics.

Of course, the novelist finds the material for his books in his own personal experience, but he must know how to transform life into a novel, for life is a novel which needs rewriting. This transformation is an extraordinarily difficult thing to do well. And how is it done? I do not know. I have never known. But I do know that when a novelist fancies he is inventing a character, he is apt to make it live because he is using life's own method. As a matter of fact, no novelist ever invents anything, but he thinks he does. There is nothing a novelist can imagine that has not already happened somewhere, at some time, in this world. But the illusion that he is really inventing carries our novelist along and forms a part of his talent, great or small.

Well, when I began writing my first book in English, I was confronted with a character that was to prove most trouble-some: the author of the book. The task that lay before me was to rewrite that character's story just as life itself had written it. This, for a novelist, is extremely difficult. His old habit of inventing is ever nagging him. 'Don't you think it would sound more plausible if you said that that hat, which was blue, was green? Don't you think that, at such and such a point, it might be well to add a little something to reality that would make it seem even more real?'

There is the novelist's temptation when he is writing about real life: to make reality seem more real by tampering with it. In a novel, to make reality seem more real than it is might be a good definition of the novelist's art, but in a book of memories, it would be tantamount to lying.

To tell the truth in an honest, simple manner is not always easy, that is, in books, but I believe that only a novelist can fully realize this. No matter how great the author's regard for truth may be, he has to cope with that giant, imagination. The character I was dealing with was particularly unmanageable. That character was the person I had been myself, and when I tried to lead him around, as one does with a character in a novel, he balked and complained to my memory, being sure that my memory would always be on his side. Memory has so little imagination. I once or twice felt like disregarding what memory had to say about facts, because I fancied that what I could imagine would be more amusing than the actual facts, but as I was writing a book of memories, I checked that impulse.

Not so long ago, in New York, I met a Frenchman who had attended Janson, the Lycée Janson. Generations of Parisians have studied there, but its greatest claim to glory, in my eyes, is that a little man with large pointed ears and a small pointed beard taught there in 1882 and 1883, his name being Stéphane Mallarmé. To go back to the man who had attended Janson at about the same time as I, he looked at me rather frigidly, I thought, and said: 'I have read your book.' He was referring to my book of memories. I returned as steady a look as I could manage and wondered what he was going to say. 'I, too, knew Mlle Blondeau.' Thus did he begin. Mlle Blondeau was the lady who taught us to read at Janson. Since that time, wars had been lost and won, revolutions had changed the face of the world, kings had disappeared from the Gotha, numberless inventions which we ingenuously mistake for progress had completely changed our way of living; it could truly be said that greater alterations had occurred since 1906 than between the days of Cromwell and those of the French Revolution, and here I stood in the presence of a man who said: 'I, too, knew Mlle Blondeau'. It made me feel dizzy, and very ancient. He went on: 'My impression is that, in the portrait you made of her, you somewhat ...' Here he made a vague gesture, which probably meant: you amplified and arranged your facts. My memory immediately protested, and I distinctly heard its voice telling me that I neither amplified nor arranged anything, that Mlle Blondeau did give two candy drops to very good pupils, one candy drop to fairly good pupils, and slapped the lazy one's faces. I said this, I said it firmly, and the man who had known Mlle Blondeau held his peace, but I am not sure he remembered the candy drops. There was a doubt in his eye. However, what made no doubt either in his mind or in mine was that that character in my book was as real to us as flesh and blood can be.

Strange to say, the only character that seemed at times a little uncertain was the author. He had a way of disappearing and I would look for him in vain, and when I did find him again, I could not see him very well. At other times, he would come quite close to me and we would look each other straight in the eye, but nevertheless like two strangers. I felt that he did not understand me completely and that he suspected me of not understanding him at all. That was because he belonged to a world that was no longer mine. How can 1940 judge and

understand 1920? Too many things are between us, things the
memories of which are fading.

We are, all of us, made up of a series of characters that don't
always feel like shaking hands with each other, characters that
go back on each other, sadly, shamefully, sometimes. Perhaps
the man of 1940 would have disappointed the younger man of
1920. We can easily imagine a dialogue between the two. How
disdainful the young man might prove: 'What? Is that all you
have accomplished in the space of twenty years? I hoped for
more, I can't say that I admire you.' And can't you hear the
older man's answer, his embarrassed explanations: 'You can't
understand. You are still too young. There were enormous
difficulties in the way.'

This aspect of the conflict between generations is one of the
trials which the author who writes about himself has to endure,
but it is a stimulating one, and when all is told, I believe it is the
greatest profit that a man derives from his own work, when he
sets about to tell readers about his own life. He discovers among
other things how little he knows about that stranger he calls
himself.

Life and Death of a Poet

Julian Green had a close friendship with Charles Péguy. Green's German publisher Kurt Wolff had fled to the United States in 1940 to found the prestigious publishing house Pantheon Books. As he did not have a new novel, Julian Green agreed to translate the poetry of Charles Péguy while his sister Anne Green translated the prose. This essay was published in 1943 as an introduction to *Basic Verities* by Charles Péguy.

There are so many things to be said about Charles Péguy, in 1942, that it seems difficult to decide how or where to begin. A few years ago, I think that it might have been much easier, I mean that I should have treated him simply as one of France's greatest modern poets, but since the downfall of this country, his name has taken on a new significance. Thousands of Frenchmen have come to him in their present distress, they have come to him for help although he has been dead for twenty-eight years, because they feel the spiritual actuality of his message. He believed in France and died for her on the battlefield of the Marne, and I doubt that any poet has ever spoken for France as he did.

It is always an ungrateful task to try to sum up a man's character in a few words, but in the case of Charles Péguy, much will have been said when we have stated that he was a Catholic and a patriot, because he was one as much as the other and he was both intensely.

Charles Péguy was born on January 7, 1873, at Orléans, the city where Bishop Saint Aignan stopped Attila in the sixth century and where Joan of Arc rallied the forces of France nine hundred years later. There was nothing very exalted about Péguy's family. His mother made a hard living by mending chairs after her husband's death which occurred when their son was still a baby. Péguy was very proud of his humble origins and when he was a grown man with college degrees and one of the masterpieces of French literature among his manuscripts, he was fond of helping his mother mend her chairs and boasted that he did it as well as anyone in the land. He called himself a peasant and insisted that French peasantry represented what was best in France. When an old French peasant speaks, the race itself speaks through his lips, and the nearer you are to that peasant, the nearer you are to the heart of real France. So reasoned Péguy.

We know very little about his childhood, but the little we know is significant enough. He attended a grammar school at Orléans and went to catechism classes where, apparently, he did very well, for M. Bardet, the curate of his parish, asked him one day if he did not wish to become a priest. The answer was quick and uncompromising: 'No,' said the child, 'that is not what I have in mind.'

When he was twelve, he was sent to the lycée at Orléans as a scholarship student, and in 1891, having passed both his baccalauréat examinations, he went to Paris in order to prepare for the Ecole Normale. From what he said in later years, it appears that at this period of his life he had lost all belief in the immortality of the soul. He entered the Lycée Lakanal, at Sceaux, in the suburbs of Paris, and one year later failed in his entrance examinations for the Ecole Normale. Possibly as a result of this setback, he decided to enlist, that is, he joined the colors a year before he would normally have been required to do so.

In 1893, he was free from military obligations and, with the Ecole Normale still in his mind, he entered the Lycée Sainte-Barbe, one of the oldest schools in Paris, and attended in its early days by such distinguished men as John Calvin and Saint Ignatius Loyola. It was at Sainte-Barbe that Péguy met some of the men who were most helpful to him in later times. There was something so compelling about his personality that the more serious of the students in his class came instinctively to him, as if for guidance.

He was on the small side but very robust and a little heavily built. His brown eyes had a way of suddenly flashing when ideas struck him, they were the bold, forceful eyes of a master. His beautiful and delicately formed hands crushed your own in their powerful grasp. When he spoke, there was immediate silence and everyone listened. Why or how this young man of twenty exercised such authority remains as mysterious as genius itself. He was serious to the point of austerity, discountenancing any form of levity such as gambling or drinking, and apparently untouched by carnal desire. There was something of the reformer about him, a gospel-like singleness of heart together with the obstinacy of a peasant and a boundless ability to take pains.

What he spoke of more often was what he called the City of the Future or, at times, the Harmonious City. In the City of the Future, there was to be no more misery, because injustice would no longer exist. There would be no rich people, because only poverty is holy, poverty, not misery, not destitution, as he carefully pointed out, Franciscan poverty, or better, socialist poverty. There would, of course, be no priests of any kind, because in those days, Péguy was an atheist and anything that smacked of religion was extremely suspicious to him. When a man's brain begins to deteriorate, it is as likely as not that he will go back to saying his prayers. So thought Péguy and so thought his friends who walked by his side, up and down the courts of Sainte-Barbe, building and perfecting the City of the Future with stones made of words.

So completely absorbed was this singular young man by his dreams that he paid little attention to the books that were being written in his day. He read Hippolyte Taine and Ernest Renan, regretting in the latter a senile tendency to believe in God. He knew a large number of Hugo's poems by heart but was never known to have read more than fifteen or twenty of Baudelaire's marvelous lines. On examination mornings, he would ask the student next to him to wake him up in thirty minutes, after he had read the theme of the composition to be handed in. Then he would go to sleep as soundly as a child and upon being awakened would immediately set to work; and exactly on the dot, he turned in a flawless paper which almost always got the highest grade. There was never the slightest mistake in what he wrote and never a correction. Péguy did not believe it was right to make corrections. Whatever went through his mind in connection with the subject was immediately couched in that straightforward style which was already so convincing. Why, he thought, should he turn down a word or a group of words that had come to him as he wrote? They had a right to stand with all the other words on the page. They expressed something in him. He wasn't going to betray them by pretending that they never had been in his mind. So down everything went on the sheet of paper.

There was much of the peasant left in Péguy. In Paris, this heaviness of his marked him as an outsider, a *provincial*; years of Parisian life could never make a Parisian of him, nor was he at all desirous of becoming what people imagine a Parisian should be like. His main preoccupation was how to better the world, how to rid people of their silly ideas about religion and make everyone a good socialist with no tommy-rot about heaven or the after-life. Once or twice a week, he and his little band of friends, you might almost say his disciples, hunted out the poor at the Butte-aux-Cailles or at the Glacière and fed them; as many as two hundred down-and-outs were given warm soup on regular days, but this act of charity could not satisfy Péguy's ambition: he wanted to do away with all destitution. At school, he was constantly asking his comrades for money, money for workers on strike; there was always a strike somewhere and money had to be obtained immediately; Péguy saw to it that Sainte-Barbe gave the proper amount. Somehow, it seemed impossible to refuse Péguy anything. He did not beg nor demand, he merely asked, but it was obscurely felt that saying no to Péguy was almost as bad as saying no to a saint.

In 1894, he left Sainte-Barbe and entered the Ecole Normale Supérieure where his old friends soon joined him. This school, as will be remembered, was founded in 1795 for the training of university professors. There was an atmosphere of intellectual fanaticism at the Ecole Normale which was exactly suited to Péguy's temper. Generally speaking, the student body fell into two groups called, in student jargon, the *talas* and the *antitalas*, the talas being the believers, and the antitalas the atheists.

Sometimes a tala would share his room with an antitala and, although they might argue fiercely, they were friends. Thus, in the same room lived a student, François Laurentie by name, who had an ivory crucifix on his desk, and a student called Talagrand who gave himself the proud title of God's personal enemy. Whenever a storm broke out, God's personal enemy would rush to the library and come back with a volume of Voltaire which he read out loud to the accompaniment of thunder and lightning. Péguy was, perhaps, no less of an atheist, but he must have frowned on God's personal enemy for his lack of poise.

He was busy writing a thesis on Kant and social duty and was in as serious a mood as ever. He was also writing something else which he seldom mentioned, the manuscript of which was locked up in a small black trunk; on the top of the trunk, a piece of paper had been pasted bearing these words written in a faultless hand: 'Please do no touch.' The only thing definitely known in connection with the manuscript (which may have been begun at Sainte-Barbe) was that Péguy devoted much time to the study of Vallet de Viriville, who wrote a history of Charles VII, and that he was more and more interested in Joan of Arc.

As time went on, however, Péguy slowly realized that he was not fitted for a university career, probably because he was now conscious of his power as a writer and found it difficult to reconcile the creative urge and the task of teaching. In December 1895, he asked M. Perrot, the director of the Ecole Normale, for a prolonged leave of absence and returned to Orléans with a threefold purpose in mind: to found a socialist center, to learn printing, and to work on his book in more propitious surroundings. By November 1896, at the beginning of the school session, he was back in his room at 'Normale'. But hardly had a few months elapsed when again he walked into M. Perrot's office and asked for another leave of absence. This time, he wanted to marry. M. Perrot was dumbfounded:

examinations were practically at hand, and here was Péguy
asking for leave of absence to get married. But Péguy insisted
that he would come back and pass his examinations the
following year. 'You will fail,' prophesied M. Perrot. Nevertheless, Péguy left school then and there.

The story of his marriage, as told by Jerôme and Jean
Tharaud, who were his school-mates, is so strange that it would
challenge our powers of belief, were it not for our knowledge of
Péguy's unusual conception of moral obligations. It shows how
mysterious the most reasonable of men can be at times.

Péguy had a very good friend called Marcel Baudoin, also
one of his school-mates. We know very little about Marcel
Baudoin who seems to have been remarkable chiefly for his
great devotion to the future poet, although the problem of his
influence over Péguy has never quite been elucidated. In July
1896, Baudoin died while he was doing his military service at
Dreux, and, as far as one knows, died of natural causes. Péguy,
however, had other views on the subject. To leave one's friends
in this way was a sort of betrayal of friendship, and Baudoin
would never have betrayed his friends, he must have been
killed. By dint of pondering over this matter, Péguy finally
came to the conclusion that Baudoin had died in consequence
of ill-treatments at the hands of a non-commissioned officer. So
one evening he took the train for Paris and at dawn the next day
he went straight to the house of his friends, woke them and said:
'Come, we are going to Dreux.' The two friends did not argue.
They got up, dressed, and the three men boarded the first train
for Dreux. In the train, Péguy explained that he was going to
kill the man whom he considered guilty of Baudoin's death.
Two swords and two pistols had been brought along for the
duel, and Péguy's friends were to be his seconds. They didn't
protest or try to reason with him, because they knew that you
could no more reason with Péguy than you could with a
pyramid. Having reached Dreux, an hour or two later, they
made for the barracks and were soon face to face with the man

whom Péguy wished to kill. He spoke quietly and it soon became obvious, even to Péguy, that he was almost as distressed as Péguy himself over the death of Baudoin, and just as innocent.

It may have been then that he made up his mind to marry Baudoin's sister in order to take the dead man's place in the Baudoin family. Mademoiselle Baudoin had some ideas in common with Péguy. To begin with, she was, like him, a revolutionary socialist. When he proposed to her, she agreed to become his wife, and in October 1897, they were married. Thus, according to Péguy's mode of thinking, was a grievous wrong partially righted. He was determined that death would not thwart him and that the spiritual link of friendship between him and Baudouin would not be severed. What mysterious logic was at the back of his conduct is difficult to grasp, but we shall see that he did not, even then, consider himself quit of the shade of Baudoin.

In November 1897, we find him again at 'Normale'. At that time, Henri Bergson was teaching at the old school and so were Joseph Bédier and Romain Rolland. The ideas they expressed were discussed as ideas are always discussed by Frenchmen, feverishly. But apart from that, there were other causes for excitement in the Latin Quarter at the turn of the century. Some years before, the Jewish captain Dreyfus had been arrested on a charge of treason which later turned out to be imaginary. In 1897, the whole case was to be retried. It would take many pages to tell about the Dreyfus case. Suffice it to say that the whole country was being aroused and divided by the issue at stake, dangerously aroused and dangerously divided. Some people contended that, even if Dreyfus were innocent — which they denied — it would be more expedient to condemn him rather than aspersions to be cast on a military tribunal and also because certain military secrets of great importance to the national defense were involved; but there were others, many others, who insisted that, Jew or no Jew (and that had a great deal to do with it), if Dreyfus was innocent, he was to be freed immediately. And of course, Péguy, with his passion for justice, was very loud in clamoring for the Jewish captain's release.

Péguy had always lamented the fact that he lived at a time when history had come to a sort of standstill. Nothing seemed to happen. To use his own words, he was living in a *period* instead of living in an *epoch*, and that, to him, was a source of worry and humiliation. He longed for the days when the heart of France beat fiercely and heroically, as it did, for instance, in 1793. 1898 seemed absurdly tame and humdrum in comparison. But now, with an innocent man being accused of an unspeakable crime, things seemed to be stirring again; it was like the first mutterings of a terrific storm, and if a man wished to take shelter, that man's name was not Charles Péguy. So, wrapped in his long dark cape that made him look like a pilgrim, with a heavy stick in his hand and his pince-nez on his nose, he led his friends into the fray. He did what all Frenchmen do when they are really excited, he went down into the street. *Descendre dans la rue*, to go down into the street, is a favorite French phrase. When Frenchmen go down into the street, the world soon knows about it. In 1789, in 1830, in 1871, they went down into the street, and now, in 1898, he, Charles Péguy, was going down into the street with his friends. A great moment. The end of a period, perhaps, and the beginning of an epoch. And where did they go? They went up and down the Boulevard Saint-Michel vociferating against the 'anti-Dreyfusards'. They marched into cafés where 'anti-Dreyfusards' met. Heavy beer glasses flew in all directions, bottles of fizzy water known as siphons were hurled and exploded, noses bled and countless arrests were made. Péguy took all this very seriously. Had he then used the vocabulary which was to become so familiar to him in later years, he would have said that, by keeping Dreyfus in jail, France was persisting in a state of mortal sin. It was too early for him to speak thus, and yet something was going on in his mind or in his heart; indeed something was always going on in those regions, but this time it was something which even his well-trained Latin brain could not quite fathom.

Perhaps Joan of Arc had a little to do with this. She had always been fond of brave, resolute and stubborn Frenchmen, and here was a Frenchman according to her heart, even though he was an atheist. He might well have fought under her white and blue banner. He was as much of a peasant as she was, and like her, he was not afraid of a broken skull.

During all this time, the manuscript was still in the little black trunk with 'Please do not touch' keeping guard over it better than any lock could have done, for who would have dared to open Péguy's trunk? The manuscript was about Joan of Arc. In fact, it was a drama about Joan of Arc, a drama divided into three plays. How strange to be writing a drama about Joan of Arc at a time where people's preoccupations were of the coming revolution, particularly when one thought of oneself as a revolutionary! But the most self-conscious among us are capable of delusions about their real nature. The play was completed in 1897, and its title made known to Péguy's admirers. A chill of disappointment must have run down their backs. Joan of Arc! A fifteenth-century saint chockfull of visions and old-fashioned ideas about right and wrong ... They were even more disconcerted when they were allowed to read the play. Nevertheless it was Péguy's book, and that was enough. What Péguy did was all right. Now came the almost impossible task of having the book published. Péguy had no money and the then enormous sum of two thousand francs had to be raised. Péguy assembled his friends and explained. They didn't argue, they didn't refuse, because Péguy's most unreasonable requests could not be refused and in December of that year the book was printed. Its size alone was impressive: an octavo numbering seven hundred and fifty-two pages. As for the chances of producing such a play on the stage, they were as slight as the play was long; it would have taken the better part of a whole day to give it. Very characteristic of Péguy was his insisting on having a list printed at the back of the book with the names of all the men who had taken a part in the manufacturing of this ponderous volume: printers, readers, correctors, compositors. What bothered him most was that he had not been able to find out the names of the men who had actually made the metal characters and those who had fished out of trash cans the rags used in making the paper. Eight hundred copies were deposited in a socialist bookstore, where they peacefully went to sleep. Then, after many weeks, something happened which startled everyone: a copy was sold.

One of the oddest features of this work was the large number of blanks left in the text. These, Péguy explained, were to be filled in later, but he failed to say how. Such as it is, the drama is little read nowadays, probably because it has been superseded by the *Joan of Arc* which Péguy wrote in later years. 'I could write about Joan of Arc for twenty years,' he once said. As a matter of fact, he wrote about her fifteen or sixteen years of his life. His first *Joan of Arc*, in spite of its awkwardness and its tendency to stand still when we should expect it to go ahead, is a very moving play, partly because of Joan of Arc whose story is faithfully told, partly because of Péguy whose genius is already recognizable. Even though we are too often reminded of a carefully written school composition, it is undeniable that a tremendous personality is foreshadowed.

As has before been hinted, it would be going too far to say that, when this first *Joan of Arc* was published, Péguy was already a Christian, although even a not very intuitive observer might have sensed that a complete change of heart was bound to take place in Péguy, sooner or later. Péguy himself was most probably unaware of this. As late as 1905, he refused to print such a hackneyed phrase as: 'God grant that such and such a thing may happen,' because of its Christian, or at any rate, theistic implications, and it was not until 1908 that he declared himself a Catholic. Nevertheless, the fact remains that he chose

Joan of Arc as the subject of his first book, the first part of which, at least, reads like a mystical poem on human suffering and salvation. We are still very much in the dark as to the psychology of conversions. When and how is a conversion brought about? In the case of Péguy, I am somewhat of the opinion that he was providentially influenced by his own work. He had not yet written what lay deepest in him — what lies deepest in us is very often beyond our ken until we go through the struggle to express it, and then it begins to react on us — but in the early scenes of this first *Joan of Arc*, he comes very close to a personal experience of Christian spirituality. And then, broadly speaking, a man who loves Saint Francis and Joan of Arc as he did and who, moreover, delights in feeding the poor, is a Christian whether he knows it or not.

One has the impression, when reading about Péguy's spiritual difficulties, that as early as 1897 he had an inkling of the crisis to come and that he instinctively shrank from it — instinctively but not consciously — as we are all apt to do when we feel that new problems are about to complicate our lives. There were plenty of complications in store for Péguy. To begin with, the socialist revolution had to be brought about. Also, the daily bread had to be earned. Many plans were agitated. Finally, it was decided that a socialist bookshop would be opened with the financial help of Mme Péguy who owned the then rather large sum of 40,000 francs. A store was found and the bookshop solemnly inaugurated in the spring of 1898, May 1st, the day of leftist demonstrations being, of course, chosen as the date of that event.

Four months later, Péguy who was then completing his third year at 'Normale,' failed at his final examinations, exactly as M. Perrot had predicted, and abandoned all plans for a university career.

To go back to the bookshop, it was situated in the heart of the Latin Quarter, only a few steps from the Panthéon, in the rue Cujas. It was very small and always very crowded, not, alas, by people who came to buy books, but by people who came in to talk, to discuss the Dreyfus case or the coming revolution, that famous 'Grand Soir' which was perpetually casting its lurid glow over the conversations of those days, or that equally famous Grand Sweeping Up, *'le Grand Coup de Balai'* which I have heard of ever since I was a boy, but have yet to witness. Such as it was, Péguy thought of his little bookshop as the stronghold of socialism, 'pure' socialism. The books were kept by a man whose face was almost impossible to see because of a beard which grew up to his eyes, or better, up to his pince-nez. (It was a pince-nez period.) Errands were run by a lame eccentric called Etienne who hopped about in a long white blouse reaching down to his calves. A black cat, which had adopted the *'cité harmonieuse'* as its abiding home, slept on the stacks of unsold copies of *Joan of Arc*. Once in a while, there was a little excitement: a band of royalists would smash a window in Péguy's shop, invectives were exchanged and walking sticks went into action in true 1898 fashion. There was quite an arsenal of walking sticks at the *'cité harmonieuse'*. We are apt to forget what a prominent part was played by sticks in those days. Péguy had one which his mother-in-law had given him; he was extremely proud of this object which was finally broken in two over his back by an irate policeman, at the time of Zola's trial.

However stimulating the presence of the socialist stronghold may have been to the Latin Quarter, the financial situation of Péguy's bookshop was disastrous. No one could be persuaded to buy *Jeanne d'Arc*. At last, the shop was saved from complete bankruptcy by a group of men who decided to take it over. One of these men was Léon Blum, who struggled vainly, in later years, to make France into a *'cité harmonieuse'*.

Péguy, however, felt that the shop was being taken out of his hands, and in 1901 he decided to take himself and his unsold books to other premises in the rue de la Sorbonne. Etienne, the old errand boy, was dismissed because he helped himself too freely to whatever money he found in the counter, but it was very characteristic of Péguy that he did not reproach Etienne with this little failing. Etienne was also extremely reluctant when it came to working, and on this score alone Péguy decided that he must be sent away. A formula had to be found which would at once inform Etienne of the bad news and spare his sensitiveness. Péguy could not think of anything. Finally, one of his friends hit upon what he considered a happy phrase. So Etienne was summoned and the following speech fell upon his ears: 'Etienne, we must part. It has been brought to our attention that you do not quit yourself of your duty with the necessary intensity.' And somehow, Etienne understood and left. I have mentioned this very small incident because I think it gives an idea of these people's kindness and seriousness.

Péguy's new bookstore was as austere as a monastery and a very strict discipline reigned between its walls, an almost military discipline. Indeed there always was a suggestion of the military about Péguy, and of the religious as well.

And in spite of his interest in modern politics, he was anything but a man of his time. There was a telephone in the shop, but he never touched it, he preferred to wrap himself up in his cape and cross the river rather than speak into a receiver to a friend.

His book-keeper in the rue de la Sorbonne was an old school-mate by the name of Bourgeois. Such a conscientious book-keeper as Bourgeois could never be found. He was what the French call *sérieux*. Péguy was very fond of repeating that one must be *sérieux* and Bourgeois was as serious as could be desired. At that time, Péguy had started a publishing business, the books published being written by Péguy and his friends. They came out regularly, like the issues of a magazine, and were called the Fortnightly Notebooks. Need I say that they were nearly all written in an intensely serious vein. They dealt mostly with social problems and the City of the Future and, of course, letters were exchanged between the publishers and their subscribers. Bourgeois answered these letters. He even answered letters which required no answer. He answered to say that there was no answer. Financial settlements were treated with the same thoroughness. If, for instance, the sum of two hundred and seventeen francs and twenty-five centimes was owed, the pennies were paid as well as the francs, which was naturally expected, but if the sum happened to be two hundred and seventeen francs and twenty-three centimes, the twenty-three centimes were paid, thus causing astonishment and admiration, because, as is well known, the French penny is worth five centimes, and five centimes, even in 1900, was so very small a sum that it was practically never divided. The centime as a coin was almost never used, except by Bourgeois who thought that if you owed a man two centimes, the two centimes had to be paid, and that to overlook such a debt was in itself an act of injustice.

Péguy's time was divided between his publishing firm and the writing of his own books. He wrote regularly, but he never knew what he was going to write when he sat down to his sheet of white paper. The idea of making a draught of what he wanted to express was completely foreign to him. His life was more and more like a long meditation interrupted only by conversations, sometimes impassioned arguments with his friends. Nobody could be as silent as Péguy, nor could anyone talk so much. What he wrote proceeded directly from silence but must have been colored by his talks. Not a word was ever scratched out. If a word came to him, he argued, it had as much right to be written down as all its fellow-words in the book. It was there as a witness, like a pebble on the long road he travelled. Péguy considered that what he wrote had been dictated to him. When he wanted to praise a book, or a sentence in a book, he never said: 'It is good,' he said: 'It is dictated.'

No book was ever brought out by the *Cahiers de la Quinzaine* without first having been read by Péguy. It is a well-known fact that almost every book we read, except the best editions of the

Bible, contains misprints. Misprints are, in a way, almost inevitable nowadays, because, however careful we may seem in our own eyes, most of us are in a tearing hurry (although where all this hurry is going to get us, I don't know). But there were no misprints in the books published by Péguy. A great French publisher, Edouard Pelletan, once said that Charles Péguy could be compared only to the sixteenth-century printers, who were real printers, not amateurs. We are amateurs in many ways. We are amateurs when we write, we are amateurs when we think, we are sometimes amateurs when we wage war, we are often amateurs when we pray, because we are in a hurry. Péguy was not an amateur. When he corrected a book, he did not read it, he searched for misprints, and when he said that the book had been corrected, it was corrected such as no book in France had been corrected.

While Péguy was busy laying the plans of the City of the Future, times were slowly moving and changing, even though the world was not aware that it was passing from a period to an epoch, the end of which is not yet within sight. On June 4, 1905, a German cuirassier wearing a flashy white uniform, got off a battleship and entered the city of Tangiers on the coast of Morocco. It was the Kaiser. On June 5, Charles Péguy, accompanied by his wife, went to one of the largest stores in Paris, the *Bon Marché*, and bought woolen socks, heavy underwear and other things a soldier may need who is going to the front. He did all this with his usual seriousness, prophesying that the history of his country and of the whole world was coming to a turning point. He did not fear war; he had always expected it to come and now he was ready, but there were nine more years to wait before the storm broke out, and after a few days excitement, Péguy found himself working again in a once more peaceful Paris.

The next few years of Péguy's life were marked by sadness and disillusionments of all kinds. To begin with, there was a fearful financial struggle to keep the *Cahiers* going. Some of them proved difficult reading, even when Péguy wrote the preface, which added considerably to the bulk of the volume. A number of *Cahiers* were entirely filled with Péguy's own words, bold, often indignant words in defense of the working classes and in attacks on our modern world which he hated. But the modern world cared little whether Péguy hated it or not and scarcely knew his name. There were other worries too. Péguy was strongheaded, obstinate and very jealous of the authority he exercised over his friends; as they grew older, however, admiration no longer prevented them from disagreeing with him and, in Péguy's eyes, these disagreements became acts of treason. He quarrelled with most of his friends, with Lucien Herr, with Jean-Pierre Laurens, with Psichari, Renan's grandson who became a Catholic, with Pierre Mille and André Spire, with Daniel Halévy, and he quarrelled with Jacques Maritain. To us who know the great Catholic philosopher, this seems almost incredible. Whenever an important issue was at stake, Maritain has shown an indomitable firmness of spirit and I venture to say that, if Péguy were to return to life in our distracted world, he could not be prouder of any other friend of his; but, whatever may be our reasons for admiring Maritain, it is his kindliness and humanity which have endeared him to so many. I have been told, however, on best authority, that he and Charles Péguy were reconciled in later years. Of their quarrel I shall say nothing, except that it seems to me to have been unduly emphasized by writers who were not present when the events they describe actually occurred.

One day in September 1908, Péguy had a conversation with his friend Lotte, about his many worries, when all of a sudden his eyes filled with tears and he said: 'I have not told you all. I have found faith again. I am a Catholic.' This was the outcome of a long struggle about which we know practically nothing. What went on in Péguy's soul from the time he declared himself an atheist, around '92 or '93, to the minute when he unburdened his heart to Lotte is a mystery which will probably never be solved. Nor did this conversion mean a simplifying of life's problems for Péguy. On the contrary. Only from the outside do conversions appear to simplify life's problems. A conversion does not mean that the fight is over and that peace will necessarily reign forever. In Péguy's case it meant quite the opposite. To begin with, there was the fact that he had married into a family of staunch unbelievers and that his children, two boys and a girl, were unbaptized, nor would Mme Péguy hear of having them baptized. And, of course, in the eyes of the Church, he and Mme Péguy were not married. So it was impossible for Péguy to live as a Catholic and he did not go to mass. Even to this day, we are not sure that he ever went to communion after his conversion; it is believed that he received the Sacrament a few weeks before he was killed, but his son Marcel states very definitely that this fact cannot be 'historically proved.'

What spiritual agony this must have meant to Péguy, we can only guess, and faintly guess. He prayed incessantly as he walked from one end of Paris to the other, or on the tops of 'omnibuses' with his beads in his hands and tears running down his face. We can be sure that Péguy did not pray like an amateur; he prayed with the obstinate faith of a medieval peasant, and yet here too were difficulties, for instance that sentence in the Lord's Prayer in which we beg for forgiveness was a stumbling-block to Péguy who insisted that we do not forgive those who trespass against us. But the important thing was that he had taken the step which leads from the outer darkness of atheism to the world of Christ, and the tears that ran down his cheeks may not always have been tears of grief.

Early in 1910, what Péguy had confidentially told Lotte was to be publicly avowed in a work which will no doubt make its author's name last for centuries in Catholic France. It bore a long title which reminds one of a heavy granite lintel over an ancient doorway: *The Mystery of the Charity of Joan of Arc.* Very few noticed the book, fewer still realized its importance. *The*

Mystery was published as a *Cahier* but most probably the
subscribers did not even cut its leaves. What they wanted was
Romain Rolland's clumsy books, and they tolerated Péguy
because they knew that, sooner or later, a Romain Rolland
would be sent to them. Critics hardly noticed the poem or had
little to say about it that might please the author. True, one
critic wrote that it was the greatest Catholic poem ever written
since the *Divine Comedy*, but that critic's name was Lotte, and
the article had been dictated to him by Péguy.

   The Mystery of the Charity of Joan of Arc has much in common
with the opening act of the first *Joan of Arc*, the socialist *Joan of
Arc*, as that early work is sometimes called, but in the *Mystery*,
the blanks have been filled and filled in such a way that Péguy
at once took his place among the greatest poets of his country.
The principal theme of this poem (which we might hesitate to
call a play) is the awakening of Joan of Arc's vocation. Indeed
nothing actually happens which could properly claim the name
of action, nor does anything happen in the second and third
Mysteries which followed in 1911 and 1912. On the other hand,
it does not seem possible to describe this work as a philosophical poem, because philosophical poems as a rule are not
without at least a suggestion of boredom or tedious abstract-
ness which is wholly lacking in Péguy's Mysteries. Péguy
shared with Dante the peculiar gift of clothing the metaphysical
with humanity. He had an eye for the invisible which only the
most mystical among primitives have had before him, because
he was himself a great primitive and there is nothing in
literature more suggestive of Dirk Bouts or Rogier Van der
Weyden than his vision of Mary following her son up Mount
Calvary, in *The Passion of Our Lady*.

   In trying to give, not an equivalent of some of Péguy's lines in
English, but what I hope is a faithful rendering of his meaning,
I have endeavored to preserve the great simplicity of language
which marks the original. Péguy's words are words which a
French child, or a French workman, or a French peasant could

easily understand. In fact, God the Father, as presented by Péguy in these Mysteries, speaks somewhat like an elderly French peasant well versed in his catechism, rather than like a professor who has read Saint Thomas, as we might have dreaded. His language is at times so plain that its very plainness defies translation. Of the speeches themselves, particularly those spoken by God the Father, I can only say very little. What characterizes them is a sort of supernatural common sense and an internal rhythm, a rhythm of thought which lends them majesty and pathos. There is in them a beauty of reasoning and a sort of medieval instinct, which we seem to have lost, for thinking in terms of the universe. Charity and intellect go hand in hand, intellect always ready to efface itself before charity which is, after all, nothing but a superior form of understanding. Péguy was essentially human and anything that smacked of pedantry was abhorrent to him. '*Je suis un auteur gai*,' he used to say. In consequence, his God the Father, although he is as strict a logician as a Frenchman can be, never discourages a joke, provided it is neither rude nor unkind, nor is he averse to joking himself, for his pre-eminent wisdom never stands in the way of his sense of humor.

To a French reader of 1912, Péguy's style must have caused extreme surprise. We are so used to it now that it seems almost inevitable that such a style should have been invented to express a certain form of religious emotion. Péguy had a very deep-rooted belief in the force of repetition, not idle repetition for repetition's sake, as we find it in more recent poets, not repetition of a word, or of a set of words, because they happen to please the author's ear, but repetition for the sake of clearness, repetition, also, to persuade and to convince. Péguy repeats himself, but he repeats himself as Bach does, that is, each repetition is enriched with a new meaning and adds to what has already been said. Indeed, music is almost irresistibly suggested by Péguy's monologues, not so much because of the fullness and beauty of their sound as by an impression of building which music also conveys, an impression of walls and towers being raised and arches vaulting over great heights.

The second Mystery came out in October 1911 under the title of *The Porch of the Mystery of the Second Virtue*, the second virtue being, of course, the theological virtue of hope. Here, Péguy's faith seemed to have reached its highest point. There was still anxious questioning in the first Mystery, but now, under the guidance of hope, he had rediscovered the 'way of childhood.' Less than half a year after that, the third Mystery appeared. It was called *The Mystery of the Holy Innocents* and dealt principally with what might be termed the perfection of confidence in God.

Almost complete silence greeted these magnificent poems. Criticisms had been made and, in one famous instance, doubts had been expressed as to the authenticity of Péguy's Catholicism when the first Mystery was published, but now, remembering the poet's furious retorts in 1910, the professional critics held their peace. The public hardly suspected that Péguy existed, and smart people who knew about books read Anatole France and d'Annunzio.

Nevertheless, Péguy kept on. His forebodings of an early death were more and more frequent and yet, he said, he must not die. There was still a tremendous number of things to be written about. Paradise for instance. He wanted to write a poem on Paradise, but not like Dante's, he explained. Péguy's ambition was to fill his Paradise with all the things he considered worth saving, Notre Dame of Paris and Notre Dame of Chartres among others, to say nothing of countless villages of France and all the tools which hard-working humanity has used since the beginning. No doubt he would also have found room for one or two of those chairs which his mother mended so well. But he did not have time to indulge very much longer in what has been called his delirium of enumeration. His last long poem, *Eve*, was published in December 1913. Its main theme is the salvation of the human race and in many respects it is a very great piece of work, but I do not think many people have read it in its entirety at one or even two sittings, not that its length might deter a serious reader, but repetitions occur with an almost maddening frequency and only slight variations of meaning. I have often had the book in hand and have invariably closed it with mixed feelings of admiration and alarm. It has the hypnotic force of an incantation. '*Ah, les mots, mon vieux, les mots!*' Péguy used to say to his friends. No one ever loved the beauty of words more than he did, and here we see him intoxicated with his own words. His often quoted lines about death on the battlefield lay buried in this gigantic poem for several years before they were discovered and first applied to him; they did much for his present fame.

Péguy's conversion did not draw him away from humanity, as so frequently happens. To begin with, he did not want to be called a convert. He had never really changed. He had become what he was, he had never ceased to belong to the old France of his peasant ancestors, and their faith was his faith. Like Joan of Arc herself, he could recite (almost) The Lord's Prayer, and Hail Mary, and the Creed, and the long litanies with their heavenly repetitions. But the dream of a world revolution was not forgotten: it was merely transferred to a higher plane. Péguy knew very well that the Church is, in its essence, revolutionary, that one of its many tasks on earth is to over-throw the old pagan order, still so very firmly established in this world. When Saint Francis preached on the holiness of poverty, he was a far greater revolutionist than Lenin, but he had no blood on his hands except the blood of the stigmata. Charles Péguy never gave up the hope of a blessed revolution whereby all bad men would be turned into good men, and poverty would be honored, and peace prevail. These dreams may seem some-what pathetic to us, in 1942, but we must not forget that man has always believed in them, that they are at the base of the teachings of the prophets, that they shine through the pages of the New Testament, and that when they seem very remote or even ridiculous, it merely means that our conscience is being obscured by some shocking crisis like the one we are going through now.

One year before he was killed, Péguy's faith was put to a test. One of his sons fell desperately ill with typhoid fever and there seemed to be little hope of saving him. Péguy did what a medieval Frenchman would have done, because he was a medieval Frenchman, he spoke earnestly to Our Lady about his unbaptized children, one of whom was in danger of death. He could not look after them. 'I have enormous responsibilities,' he explained to the Queen of Heaven. 'You must do something for my children. I place them in your lap, I give them to you, and now I am going away before you can give them back to me.'

The sick child recovered. 'Naturally', said Péguy who showed no surprise (he knew how to ask).* However, he had promised Our Lady of Chartres to make a pilgrimage to her church if his child was saved, but he was not in a hurry to redeem his promise; he was never in a hurry about anything. Several months went by, then he put on his heavy shoes, took his stick and started out on foot in the direction of Chartres. There are seventy-two kilometers between Paris and Chartres and it took Péguy three days to cover that distance. He left us an account of his pilgrimage in a poem which, by a caprice of fate, brought him something like recognition a few months before he died.

When the war broke out, Péguy was forty-one and should normally have been in the reserve, but to a man of his type, this was simply unacceptable. Early in August, he left for the front with his regiment, having been given the rank of lieutenant. There was no mistake about it this time: he was living, at last, in an epoch. All during the harrowing month of August, the

---

* Later his children were baptized. His wife became a Catholic after his death.

German armies swept through Northern France until they were stopped, in the first week of September, along the river Marne. Péguy's regiment was in the neighborhood of Senlis. On the third of September, they were quartered for a few hours in a deserted convent. Péguy spent that night decorating the altar of Our Lady with flowers which he had picked. On the fourth, he and his men moved on in the direction of Meaux. On the fifth, in the early part of the afternoon, they were in the neighborhood of Villeroy with shells bursting all around them. The men ran a few yards forward, then stopped and threw themselves on the ground to shoot at the already retreating Germans. But Péguy did not lie down. There he stood in his red and blue uniform, a living target in the blazing sun, telling his men to shoot at will, then running ahead of them to lead them on. They all shouted to him to lie down, but he, with an oath, told them to keep on shooting. The last thing he probably saw was the German line wavering and falling back. A bullet struck him in the forehead and he fell with a groan as his men ran to victory. When they looked for his body after the battle was over, they had some trouble in identifying it, but a friend of his finally succeeded in doing so: he found a coin in one of the dead man's pockets, a one centime piece, one of Bourgeois's centimes.

Blessed are those who died in great battles,
Stretched out on the ground in the face of God ...
Blessed are those who died in a just war,
Blessed is the wheat that is ripe and the wheat that is
                                        [gathered in sheaves.

Thus wrote Péguy, in 1913, under the dictation of his prophetic soul.

A Steamer Letter

Written in 1945, this essay was published in the January 4 issue of *Commonweal* in 1946.

The ship, the sea, the sky are all of the same color: dark gray. My thoughts too are gray! I have been thinking of you as never before. Perhaps this sounds a little strange, almost embarrassing, but I want you to know. Three years ago, I stood alone by a window, in Baltimore. There was nothing but desolation in my heart then, as I looked at the bare trees standing stark and black against the steel blue sky; it was a sky such as I had never seen in Europe: somehow it seemed farther away from the earth. At that moment, a voice inside me spoke very surely and said: 'The day will come when you will go back to France.' I knew it was true even though it seemed unbelievable at the time, and I tried to imagine that day, the scurrying about for passports and tickets and reservations, the packing, the farewell parties, everything a little frantic with a great effort on my part not to appear too happy. But of course I did not know you then.

I am not forgetting that we had met before, but you weren't very often in my mind. Even when we talked and I looked at you, I realize that I talked and looked in an absent sort of way, I mean that there was always a part of me that wandered off. Shall I go on? Years went by and you were there, you were always there. At times, I found it gratifying to go to my room and close my door in order to be alone, but you had a way of being with me just the same. We lived together, in the same place, under the same roof.

Circumstances had brought that about. I became accustomed to your presence. We were, after all, of the same blood. There were things, secret things, secret ways of feeling which we had in common, they were almost like family secrets and when I looked at you, I was often reminded of my mother. Nevertheless I contemplated leaving you with perfect equanimity! I had to go and I wanted to go.

So the day came when I was told that I could leave, and exactly as I had foreseen, there was much rushing about in

Washington for passports and tickets, much sitting on trunks that couldn't close, and, to be sure, a farewell party. The picture was complete, in a way. I alone realized that something was wrong. I had had an inkling of it some weeks before, so suddenly that it startled me; then back and back it came with tireless pertinacity. I awoke at night and stayed awake thinking of you, remembering things you had said.

A few days ago I boarded this ship. There was a drizzle over New York, then a mist. All around me French voices made a sort of hum, the hum I had not heard for years, and it moved me. The clear, quick speech spoke of many things I loved and hoped to find again, but I talked to no one; I gave the harbor a hasty glance and was shown to my cabin where I crept into my bunk. After a while the voices grew to a higher pitch of excitement, I could hear them distinctly together with the patter of feet over my head: '*Venez vite! On part, venez voir!*' I didn't move, however, I know exactly what New York looks like with its lights gleaming through the evening mist. I did not realize, three years ago, that things would happen quite this way. I lay quite still. There was a throb like that of a big heart, and with my face to the wall I listened to it as we pulled out of the harbor, and something in me measured the growing distance between us, and I thought of you, America.

How a Novelist Begins

First published in *Atlantic Monthly*, December 1941, this essay formed part of the material for a literature course which Julian Green gave at Princeton University in April 1941. By this time he had published eight novels in French which were all translated into English.

There are many things that a novelist learns by writing novels, but this knowledge does not seem to be transmissible; it is something that has to be acquired at a great cost and cannot be left in a will. I have often wondered why. If I were a watch-maker and talked to people who happened to be interested in watches, I suppose that I should derive some pleasure from taking a watch to pieces, metaphorically at least, simply to show these people its inner structure, but nothing of the sort can be done in the case of a novel, because a good novel is not a piece of machinery with wheels and springs, all producing the desired effect at the right moment; a good novel is a living organism, and when you take a living organism apart and put it back together again, all you have is something dead.

Of course, some novels can be dealt with like clocks and watches. An expert critic can pick them apart, name all the intricate little bits of steel and explain their movement, then readjust all the hairlike springs and infinitesimal wheels, wind up the watch, give it a shake or two, and the watch, being con-structed according to rules, behaves the way a watch is supposed to behave: it ticks and the critic feels proud because he has made clear the secret workings of that particular watch, and the watch runs, and the book sells, and everybody is pleased.

I believe there are infallible methods of constructing such books as the ones I have in mind in a way that will prove commercially lucrative, but I do not think that a born novelist can really be interested in these mechanical feats of ingenuity. Few novelists have been as awkward as Balzac, or Emily Brontë, or Conrad, or Marcel Proust. They proved more than once indifferent watchmakers, but this distinction can be made between their novels and, let us say, 'clever' novels: the latter emit a thin, regular, and, to some ears, immensely satisfactory ticking, whereas the former throb from page to page with the beating of the human heart.

A curious sound, the beating of a heart, a sound which

cannot be imitated in books and which only living books can give, nor can I think of any rule for writing a living book other than 'Be alive and your book will live'. It seems to me, however, that something a little more definite can be said on the subject. About ten or fifteen years ago a French journalist interviewed a certain number of writers and asked them the following question: 'Why do you write?' It was an impertinent question, and, like a great many impertinent questions, a very penetrating one. Dr. Johnson said on one occasion that nobody but a fool would write for anything but money. No such answer was given by any of the writers interviewed, although quite a few, I believe, might have endorsed Dr. Johnson's bold and clean-cut statement. They thought of pleasing intellectual reasons which they dressed up in fine words, and, having successfully evaded the question, mentally mopped their brows. But the question remains, and should keep any man awake who is about to begin a novel.

Very few could give the only possible answer, which is: 'I write because I was born to write, and if I do not write I cannot live. To be sure, I can breathe and sleep and overeat like other people, but I cannot really live if pen and paper are taken away from me forever. It matters little whether I be rich or poor; I carry something in my heart which must be expressed.'

If all living authors were suddenly presented with very large sums of money by, let us say, prosperous lunatics, there would be a dearth of novels in the coming years. This, I am afraid, would be the test of many but not all spurious talents. 'Would you write if you were rich?' is a question which should turn away droves of authors from the literary pastures, but I can think of another question which should be asked the obstinate few: 'Would you write if you were alone, for instance, on a desert island, with a lot of paper and all the ink you needed?' Or 'Would you write if you lived among people who could not read?' 'Would you write if your writings were invariably jeered at?' And this last and more searching question: 'Would you write if you could never get into print?'

To write without any prospect of seeing one's writings in print would no doubt be as tiresome as perpetually talking to oneself for lack of anyone else to talk to. We need an audience, we need appreciation and critism, we need a certain amount of opposition (a lot of that is given free). The welcome, warm or cold, extended to an author's first book is bound to have some kind of influence on the second book. Should the welcome be too warm, the second book stands in fair chance of being born lame and constitutionally weak. Should the reception of the first book be rude and unfair, a loud, defiant second book may come into the world.

I suppose vanity is at the bottom of all this. The urge to write is very fine in itself, but the urge to write without being admired, what of that? Does it exist? We may doubt it, and yet a man can write a book simply because he feels that if he does not he will burst, and he may write it knowing very well that all the public he can ever count on having is himself; or he can write a book which will demand years of toil and burn it, like Gogol.

All of which, however, does not mean that great books have not been written for the sake of money or for the sake of admiration. Balzac produced a number of novels to pay his debts, and Racine proudly said that he wrote for fame; but Balzac would have written as much had he been a millionaire, and Racine had he been totally unsuccessful, because they had in them this driving force which produces plays, novels and poems. On the other hand, I believe that if Balzac had been prevented from writing, he would have been, as the saying goes, fit to be tied, whereas Racine under the same circumstances would have died of melancholia; but I do not think that there are many authors in this or any other country who would run the same risk, should, let us say, unhappy circumstances compel them to give up their profession.

A writer is not a loafer: a writer works as hard as any business man; a writer toils; a writer feels sometimes, like Carlyle, that

his brain is made of mud, yet he must go on because that which
is in him must be expressed.

There is something very exhilarating about writing the first
lines of a novel. They contain a promise which may or may not
be fulfilled, the promise of a good book. Five or six lines more,
and the promise may be broken then and there, and the author
not know about it until the whole book is written. The importance of these opening sentences can hardly be overestimated.
In a way, they are the nucleus of the book, and all the other
sentences in the book are somehow the continuation of these
initial words. Baudelaire once said that you could really begin a
novel at almost any point, but that you had to begin with what
he called *des très belles phrases*, very beautiful sentences. This is
the point of view of a great artist who knew the importance of
giving tone to a piece of writing by striking the right note at the
outset. However, the real difficulty does not begin until after
the opening sentences have been written, because a number of
people are capable of writing two or three good sentences which
may serve as a fair beginning — although, goodness knows, it is
difficult enough to write a good sentence anywhere, at any time
— but precious few are capable of following up those sentences
with other sentences that will, if I may say, justify them.

So we must beware of that feeling of elation which takes
possession of us as we embark on a novel, but we must bear in
mind that the opening sentences of our book are those which
probably stand a better chance of remaining in the reader's
memory than almost any other. They are like the first glimpse
we catch of a face: the face pleases or repels, and more will be
found out about it later when it is more closely studied, but
what catches our eye in the very first seconds is what really
counts — that hasty but deep and all-informing impression will
seldom be revised in its fundamentals; and if, on closing a novel
which you have just finished, you remember the way it begins,
it may strike you how strangely prophetic of the whole book
those opening sentences were.

I can illustrate what I mean only by giving an example or two taken from famous books. One of my favorites is this:

'For a long time I used to go to bed early. Sometimes, when I had put out my candle, my eyes would close so quickly that I had not even time to say "I'm going to sleep". And half an hour later the thought that it was time to go to sleep would awaken me; I would try to put away the book which, I imagined, was still in my hands, and to blow out the light; I had been thinking all the time, while I was asleep, of what I had just been reading, but my thoughts had run into a channel of their own, until I myself seemed actually to have become the subject of my book: a church, a quartet, the rivalry between François I and Charles V.'

We may know nothing about Marcel Proust and never have read a page he wrote, but these opening chords warn us that we are listening to a man who has a great deal to say and is going to say it with infinite complexity, and with such a feeling for nuance and such a hatred of the obvious that we shall soon be wondering at the mysteries of everyday life. It is very characteristic of him to begin his huge work with the word *longtemps*, 'for a long time' because in no other book that I know has time ever been so magically brought to a standstill and the duration of things treated as a sort of element which allows as much exploring as the space in a room. So here we have a man with an almost infinite quantity of time on his hands because he is ill in bed and will be ill until he dies. A certain dreaminess is induced by this condition — not a haziness of the mind, but a new and marvelous faculty to see the world from the inside, as it were, to get at the substance of things which we glance at absentmindedly. With this man we stand on the threshold of a strange new world, and, if you will follow him through the ten or twelve volumes of his extraordinary novel, you will realize that the whole work was, as philosophers say, *in fieri* in the first half page of the first volume.

I should now like to quote the first sentence of another book.

It is a very plain sentence but it is connected in my mind with early childhood memories. When I heard it for the first time, I felt a vague and indescribable longing to make up stories of my own, to write stories, to write a book. I was about nine, and the book was the most famous novel in the English language: It began as follows: 'I was born in the year 1632, in the city of York, of a good family, though not of that country, my father being a foreigner of Bremen, named Kreutznaer, who settled first at Hull.'

What I read into this sentence, I cannot recall. Probably I was taken by the names of cities where I had never been, and also by the date, which carried one back to exciting times. Now I like the sentence for different reasons: it is bare and it rings true; it is precise with no desire to please, but rather with a wish to convince the reader of its veracity by its very artlessness. If this man is going to tell us lies — as indeed he is prepared to do during five hundred pages, because he is the most magnificent liar that ever wielded a pen — he is going to tell them in such a way as to make us stare and gape like children, for, try as we may, it is difficult to outgrow *Robinson Crusoe*.

To go back to our modern author who is enjoying the bliss of turning out a few pleasing sentences at the top of page 1 of his new novel, I think it may be as well for him to stop after having written ten or twelve lines, call it a day, and go to bed with the happy thought that he is perhaps embarking on a sensational bestseller, or even on a masterpiece. His troubles will begin on the following day when he rereads what he has written and wonders how he is going to follow it up.

Being interested in technical questions of this kind, I have asked a number of novelists to tell me how they proceeded. Some of them write out, usually at considerable length, not only the plan of their book, but the detailed plan of each chapter, so that the actual writing of the novel means no more than piecing together a large quantity of notes and polishing them up in order to give them what is called style. The polishing, I may say, takes considerable time and all the talent one can afford. Most authors, however, are content with a sketchy plan which leaves more freedom to the imagination; and some authors — but very few — go nervously ahead with no idea as to what their characters are going to do and follow them as best they can until the last page is reached.

Racine, when he had written the outline of a tragedy in about a page and a half, used to say: 'I have written my play,' meaning, I suppose, that writing out the speeches in verse was the easiest part of his task. Excellent authors believe that to begin a book without first having carefully thought out the plan is rash and unreasonable, and I allow that it is dangerous. Should an author be too unmindful of the way in which his book is to be constructed, he might very well find himself in the plight of the Italian architect who hastily built himself a house and only when the roof was up, and each door in place, realized with a pang that he had forgotten the staircase. And yet there is much to be said for those who are averse to plans and who prefer to make up their story as they go along, not knowing what the morrow will bring or how the book may end; and here, I believe, we are reaching a very essential point in the study of the novel.

It has always been my opinion that too careful a plot can kill a book, for the simple reason that it is apt to turn the characters into automatons; their task is to carry out a plot, whether they like it or not. Theirs not to reason why, theirs but to do and die, and they usually take their revenge by behaving like animated dolls. Some books are obviously written for the sake of the plot, and the characters are made to fit in as best they can. If the plot is an exciting one, the faulty or superficial psychology will not be noticed except by a few fussy specialists. The average detective story, for instance, stands or falls by the quality of its plot. The same is true of Dumas Père's novels: adventure is the theme of all his books, and characterization — a hasty, childish, Punch-and-Judy-like characterization — is thrown in like a dash of pepper in a ragout. To borrow one of E.M. Forster's phrases, his characters are flat instead of being round.

It seems plain enough, then, that the plot of a story should serve to express what is going on inside the characters. A plot by itself is as gratuitous as a fairy tale, and can be just as charming, but, in the last analysis, it is not the essential part of a book. To be sure, a novel without a plot is apt to be tiresome, and, after all, 'What is going to happen?' is a very natural question to ask one's self when reading a story, but it is a fact that the plot can dwindle to almost nothing and the story remain a good story.

The problem of thinking up a plot is one of those false problems over which much valuable time is wasted. The question is not 'Can I invent a story worth writing?' but 'Can I create characters capable of actions worth recording?' It is not the novelist who should be the author of the plot, but the characters to which the novelist's brain has given birth. Let the novelist create characters worth creating and the plot will take care of itself – that is the characters will take care of the plot. The book is their book, not the author's. If they are constitutionally strong, they will try to wrest the book from each other, or, as we say, to steal the show. Thus, it happens that characters that were meant to be of secondary importance come to the fore, by sheer vitality, and remain there in spite of the author. An excellent example of this is Sarah Gamp. The other characters and the plot of *Martin Chuzzlewit* may fade somewhat from your memory and entirely disappear in time, but Sarah Gamp will ever remain among the ruins, with her bottle of gin and her strong language.

When people describe the characters in a book as the children of the author's brain, they are seldom aware of the truth hidden in this figure of speech. I have always found it a singularly apt phrase because it seems to me that most authors treat their characters exactly as some parents treat their children — that is, they bring them into this world and expect them to obey them until they, their parents, die. It is naturally to be expected of children that they obey their parents, but if the parents live long enough, and the children grow up into men and women with ideas of their own, conflicts are bound to occur whenever parents try to enforce their views on the younger generation. As a rule, parents do not attempt this; they usually resign. Now, authors are very often like unwise parents who will not realize that their children are no longer children. 'After all,' they think, 'whose characters are these? I'll make them do exactly as I say.' So they write a nice, detailed plot even before the characters are born.

But suppose the author is really talented and, instead of creating people made of paper and ink, actually creates living people — characters that breathe and have human hearts that beat and don't tick like watches, people who think thoughts of their own and want things — something very curious is going to happen. These characters are going to obey the author for a while, until they are fully equipped mentally and physically, and then they are going to revolt and tear the plot to pieces, and nothing more fortunate can happen to any author. They are going to live their own lives because they don't care for the destiny which has been mapped out for them.

How is this going to happen? At what point of the plot will they begin to get out of hand? Only the author and a very subtle reader could say, but it may also happen that the author himself cannot tell.

I have said that nothing more fortunate could happen to an author than to see his plot taken in hand by his characters. This means that, instead of just adding another book to his list, he has actually brought living people into this world. His characters have blood in their veins, not ink. When we have turned the last page, the characters go out of the book and go on living with us. I need not tell you that this happens very seldom. The very great can bring it about sometimes, and once in a while a second-rate author does it, too, just as we see a second-rate actor who night after night plays his part wretchedly and one evening — when no one is paying attention, probably — is suddenly transfigured and for a few minutes seems to own the world. This is not a trick. People call it vaguely, but not inaptly, inspiration. And what is inspiration?

We are all familiar with the stories about Gustave Flaubert's agonies when he wrote his novels, and, in particular, *Madame Bovary*. Just a few miles from Rouen, in an old house facing the Seine, he would sit from morning until night in front of a sheet of paper on which, sometimes, only a few lines had been painfully written; several hours would go by without his stirring as much as a finger, absorbed as he was in a gigantic struggle for expression, or lost in a sort of inner contemplation of his characters. It took him five years to write his book, but time seems grateful to him for the long weary months he spent on this work, which we still read with interest and emotion.

Madame Bovary, which may well outlast almost every novel written since, affords a good example of a novel constructed around a character rather than around a plot. If you reread the book and bare the plot of all non-essentials, you will see that it is an extremely simple one, so simple that it might well be summed up in two or three sentences; its very simplicity was one of the elements in the lasting success of the book, but the book was not written for the sake of success. Flaubert was too great a writer to confuse success and fame; he wrote, like Racine, *pour la gloire* — that is, for the sake of fame. He knew his ability to write sentences which could not die, but he was a genius, and, like many geniuses, he fell short when writers of ordinary talent would have excelled. It is quite possible that a man of ordinary talent, had he had the idea of a plot like the plot of *Madame Bovary*, would have made a better story, a more exciting story, a story with a more ingeniously complicated action; but it is also possible that his book would be today as dead as a Bulwer-Lytton romance. Other novels by Flaubert suffer from — or should I say benefit by — the same lack of plot-inventiveness.

Is it that he lacked imagination? But who would dare say that one of the greatest novelists of all times lacked imagination? No, his powers of imagination were directed toward creating characters rather than developing a plot. If a child had asked Gustave Flaubert to tell him a bedtime story of his own invention, I have an idea that the novelist would have had considerable trouble in pulling through the test. Yet it was this man who probably gave away the secret of all great stories when he said of his best-known character: 'I, Gustave Flaubert, am Madame Bovary!'

How can such a thing be? Isn't it rather funny to think of Gustave Flaubert, with his bald head and long red mustaches, pretending that he is Madame Bovary? He was the son of a surgeon who had given him something of his own professional toughness. There was nothing maudlin about Gustave Flaubert. He was a man of violent passions and enormous appetite. What affinity could exist between this person, who prided himself on looking like a Norman pirate, and the provincial lady whose story he told so convincingly?

If you have read his letters, you know how strongly opposed he was to anything like a literary attitude, how ready to laugh at poseurs, how ferociously honest with himself and others. Words were not things to be used in vain; to Flaubert they were, in a way, sacred, each one to be weighed with almost fanatical care before it was spoken or written down; so that *'Madame Bovary, c'est moi!'* is not an utterance lightly to be ascribed to literary excitement. What he meant, presumably, was that by concentrating on his character he had succeeded in identifying himself with it.

This is a process well known to novelists who deserve that name, and also to actors whose methods are sometimes so curiously linked with the methods of novelists. We are all familiar with the story of the second-rate actor who so often plays the part of Napoleon that he finally comes to believe that he is Napoleon, and carries on this tiresome impersonation in his everyday life until a home is at last provided for him by the medical authorities. But the characters that actors have to deal with are necessarily static. Napoleon on the stage knows that he must be rude to the Pope, amorous with Josephine, and that he must eventually die in a narrow bed murmuring names of battles. His business is to put life into a gray coat, a black hat, whereas the novelist, who is creating a character of his own, lives a sort of second life which may be full of surprises. He is not simply animating a part; he creates with his own flesh and blood a being capable of suffering, and what happens to the character is primarily experienced by the author.

All this is more easily described than explained. Flaubert tells us in a letter that, when writing about Emma Bovary's nervous fit, he practically had convulsions himself. To work one's self up to such a pitch requires such enormous concentration that very few novelists are ready to face the ordeal. Most novelists are lazy, and therefore inattentive to the inner vision which they should try to call up. They do not see what they are writing about. They delude themselves by writing clever sentences that serve as mirrors in which they can admire their own wit, but it is impossible to read a page they have written without feeling that they never saw what they endeavor to describe. I do not mean that they never saw it in what is called real life — I mean that they did not see it while they were writing. In consequence, what they write is a mere pretense and a lie: and lies are just as tiresome in books as they are in everyday life.

In the popular conception, genius is something more or less equivalent to facility; uncanny facility as they would say now. If a man is capable of playing ten games of chess simultaneously, he is a genius. If he can paint a complete picture in thirty minutes, he is a genius, provided he sells the picture for a good price. If he can write thirty pages a day for thirty days and win a prize by doing so, he is a genius, at least for a little while. But if we live the lives of the very great, we see that genius is almost always synonymous with effort, and that, more often than not, it is unaccompanied by any kind of facility.

The result of intense concentration on the part of the novelist is the bringing up of his inner vision. The born novelist is a *seer*, and the more he believes in what he sees, the greater he is. What truth is there in fiction? Fiction, from a certain point of view, could well pass for a series of gratuitous statements concerning people who do not exist, and this definition would fit a staggering majority of novels, ancient and modern. But why quibble? The truth of fiction depends largely on the accuracy of the author's observations.

So deeply convinced of this were the naturalists of the nineties that they accumulated great masses of notes before daring to begin their novels. Whenever they saw something which they thought they might use, they scribbled a few words on a slip of paper, or, if they had none, on their shirt cuffs, and that was observation number fifty-five concerning the way the heroine carried her sunshade or blew her nose. So, piece by piece, the portrait was made up, and the extreme accuracy of every detail persuaded the author that it was as true a portrait as could be painted.

Yet, of all novels ever written, few can be more artificial than some novels of that period. This is very strange. Can it be that life is something which we are not able to photograph? Why are certain books lifeless in spite of the fact that they present a perfectly correct picture of life? Why is it that the more accurate they are, the more they seem to be telling lies? Why is it that certain novelists succeed in getting at psychological truth when they make up a story whereas they fail disastrously when they report on something they have actually witnessed?

This is the revenge of the gods. You identify fiction with lying; therefore lying — that is, inventing — will be your only means of creating something like truth. You can't empty a bagful of facts in a novel and expect them to remain true to life; they have to be transmuted into something with life in it. You can't just take a heavy portion of reality, dump it in a book, and expect it to live; it will be as dead as something fished out of the river and put on a marble slab. Life in itself cannot be copied and imitated in books; it must be recreated. A real novelist is neither a photographer nor a dreamer indulging in idle fancies; he is a man with a strange power to substitute himself for life and to create destinies. Or, if you prefer to reverse the terms of the problem, you might say that life itself is the greatest of all novelists; we cannot successfully imitate her novels, but we can learn a great deal by studying her methods.

A very uneven novelist is life, at times a very poor one, using unnecessary repetitions, heavily insisting on obvious relationships, proudly dragging in coincidences by the hair as if to say, 'Ha! You didn't expect that, did you?' But, at other moments, what superb flashes of genius, what a way of sending you back twenty-five years in the space of a second and casting light on a whole destiny by referring to an incident which the *reader* had utterly forgotten! '*Quel roman que ma vie!*' said Napoleon at Saint Helena. Most of us can say as much, if we try to think of ourselves as characters in a novel, we realize that the working out of our destinies is in the hands of a very great artist. The book may not always afford very good reading; I allow that much of it seems tiresome; but there are moments when a glimpse of the general plan is caught and the secret meaning of a dull chapter is brought to light.

Almost any writer with moderate cleverness can make up *personages* and endow them with speech of a kind, but it takes a little more than mere talent to convey the impression of an unseen force perpetually at work in the lives of these characters. This is a gift, and a rare one, not something that can be acquired by dint of hard work and determination. It is something as gratuitously bestowed as an ear for music or an eye for color. It is akin to religious feeling. Sophocles had it to an eminent degree and in our times Tolstoy. It is a sense of what is really permanent behind what passes, and we can only feel like schoolchildren in the presence of the great novelists who are possessed of this knowledge. We cannot imitate them, but we can at least try to see things from their point of view.

What is genius but a knowledge of what is going on behind the stage while the play is being performed? What is a higher form of intuition but genius? This intuition cannot be acquired any more than a gift can be acquired, but surely concentration must be a step in the right direction. Intuition is not the reward of long and patient efforts to concentrate, but concentration awakens the dormant power to understand what is hidden from most human beings.

It is sometimes said that childhood often shows traces of genius which education causes to disappear, because the object of education is to help a percentage of minds to reach a certain level, whereas some children are virtually above the average level and are, in a way, being forced down instead of being helped up. They could ascend much higher, but their innate superiority is not taken into account and they are slowly and patiently fashioned into average human beings, and by the time they are seventeen or eighteen whatever originality was in them is stamped out unless they are strong enough to fight and assert themselves. This is no fault of education. Education is made for the many, not for the few.

If we study the lives of great writers from this point of view, we shall be struck by the fact that much of the child remains in the man when the man is really great. He is so dependent on his childhood that in spite of his experience, in spite of his technical ability to write a book and fulfill his career, he is a child. He has retained the intensity of feeling of a child, he believes in his own stories as completely as a child believes in the stories told by a grown-up, he marvels at things or is repelled by them with the same whole-heartedness as a child. This is particularly true of a man like Charles Dickens, who went through life with the soul of a boy and was able to the end to draw on the magnificent imagination of childhood.

What kind of books Dickens — or, for that matter, any great novelist — might have written had the memory of his childhood been completely taken away from him by some freakish accident? Very artificial books, books lacking in anything like spontaneity and freshness. One of the most interesting traits of childhood is that it is constantly being surprised by what it sees. There are cries of admiration and wonder on the lips of every child that is taken for a drive to some new place: he is perpetually discovering the world. So it is with great novelists. Most grown-ups can yawn at the finest landscapes, whereas a born novelist will describe a tree as if he had never seen one before and will make you share his joy. When D.H. Lawrence describes a lake in Mexico, you wonder whether you have ever looked at water before. When Conrad describes a typhoon, you feel like stopping up your ears.

Do not be deceived: this is the vividness of childhood which has been retained by man.

As a rule it is not so much what a writer puts in his novels that surprises him as what he leaves unexpressed. In a way, you might compare a novel to an iceberg: one-third above sea level and two-thirds in the water; one-third emerging to the light, two-thirds plunging, as it were, in invisible depths. I think the proportion is just about right as far as the novel is concerned. The main part forms a sort of floating mass below the surface of — well, the surface of the page.

A good novelist is a novelist who, consciously or unconsciously, chooses what he is going to say. He can't say everything, for lack of time and space, if he wants the story to move on, and what he does not say is sometimes as significant as what he does say. The very essence of his talent lies in the quality of his choice. We are endeared to certain writers by their reticences; nor do I mean by 'reticence' timidity or squeamishness. There is an exquisite sense of reticence in Stevenson, and a world of unexpressed thoughts and emotions in *Dr. Jekyll and Mr. Hyde*, for instance. Another example, and perhaps a better one, is Henry James's *Turn of the Screw*, a book made dreadful by what lurks unsaid behind the characters, a book of sinister intimations; but, of course, it is impossible to suppose that such an experienced and self-conscious artist as Henry James was not aware of what he left in the dark when he wrote his appalling story. In the same way, we are bound to admit that Stevenson knew precisely what he was doing when, closing the door on Mr. Hyde, he omitted to tell us many things which curious readers might like to learn concerning that character.

To go back to our iceberg floating blindly on what a psychoanalyst might call the sea of the subconscious, I believe there are many such icebergs, floating on exactly that kind of sea in present-day literature. Some are made impressive by their size, some gleam and sparkle in the sun like diamonds, some are simply big lumps of frozen water, cold, heavy, and colorless. All, however, have this in common: much of their bulk is made up of something which we cannot see but which we know is there. What is it?

Let us try to find out. When an author writes 'Chapter I' at the top of a blank page, he is starting out on a strange and often dangerous adventure. Without knowing it always, he is going to tell us all about himself, but he feels perfectly safe because he masquerades as a dozen different people and never credits the reader with enough perspicacity to find him out. What he wishes to do or say himself, but doesn't quite dare, he makes his characters say and do in his stead. This acting by proxy gives him a great sense of freedom. At the same time, it betrays him in the eyes of those who really know how books are written. Curiously enough, an author is much more difficult to get at when he is deliberately writing about himself, because, of course, he is then on his guard. The most sincere and outspoken confession can turn out to be the most impenetrable of masks. Only when the author pretends to be someone else does he really give himself away. He is in the situation of the Emperor in Hans Christian Andersen's tales: everybody believes that he is fully clad, and he does too, perhaps, when he is really walking through the streets stark naked.

Montesquieu said that no man knew how to write well unless he knew how to skip intermediate sentences, and I remember that saying each time I look at one of the nine-hundred-page novels which are turned out nowadays.

The main bulk of our iceberg is made up of intermediate sentences; although these sentences are not actually written out on the page, their presence must somehow be felt — that is, the book must convey the impression that the author knows more than he says. An author who tells you all he knows is a bore. For that reason I shall stop now, having given away some of the secrets of my trade, but confident that they can be of use only with the help of that magic and apparently gratuitous gift — talent.

Where Do Novels Come From?

This is the text of a lecture that Julian Green gave at Goucher College, Maryland, in 1941. The English manuscript is slightly incomplete, and it is possible that the complete version is still in some archives somewhere in the United States.

Where do novels come from? One of the legitimate answers to that strange question might be: 'I don't know.' However, as it seems rather difficult for any man to explain for a whole hour that he doesn't know the answer to a question he himself has asked (and which nobody ever asked him to ask), some kind of answer must be found. Now, there are several ways of not knowing a thing. You can be totally and absolutely ignorant of the subject in question, and candidly admit it. Or you can be ignorant and pretend that you know, which is tiresome for all concerned. Or you can be ignorant with a more or less strong suspicion of the truth. To make my own position clear, I must admit that I do not know where novels come from, but I am ready to make a few guesses based on my experience as a novelist.

In asking where novels come from, we are dealing with nothing less than the problem of literary inspiration. We might as well ask where poems come from. In most cases it is impossible to say. What seems to be the starting point, if we examine it closely, is in reality a link in a chain. It is preceded by something vague and shadowy, which in its turn may well have been preceded by something even more vague and shadowy.

Before going any further, it may be well to state right here what kind of novels I have in mind. Let us suppose that a writer goes to a foreign country which happens to be in a state of revolution. The writer's idea in visiting that country is to gather information which he intends to give to the public in the form of a story. Having remained abroad for a certain length of time, he comes back, writes his book and calls it a novel. There is nothing very mysterious about the origin of such a book. It may be a very good book. It may tell a very exciting story. But it is not a novel. It is rather a piece of journalism in the guise of fiction, with characters fitted to the story, that is, characters deliberately created to fill the needs of the story. What happens in a case like this — many of the kind are written in times of war — what happens is that the story swamps the characters, or, if you prefer, that the real characters are the events themselves.

In a book written for the sake of the characters, the story is the outcome of what those characters think and do. The story itself cannot bring the characters to life. It is only an outward manifestation of what is going on inside those characters. If you insist on imposing a story on your characters, the latter will simply turn into puppets, obedient puppets. What will really count then, in the mind of your reader, is the story. He may not believe in your characters, but he will want to know what happens in the story, he will be interested in the succession and the connection of certain events; he won't care two straws about the people in your book, but he will turn over a great number of pages in order to find out just what becomes of them. This may seem a little paradoxical. Why should I be interested in knowing what becomes of a person in whom I am not in the least interested? Why? Because what happens to that person is actually more interesting than that person himself. The character is superseded by the event, to such a point that the real character is actually the event. Events are born, grow, develop and make a final exit, just like people.

Characters in novels or plays do not necessarily have to be people. They can be events, as I have pointed out, or inanimate objects, or even natural phenomena. There are a great many examples of this kind of thing. Some years ago, I saw a play by the French author Lenormand[10] in which the main character was the desert and more particularly the wind that blows across the Sahara, the simoom. The simoom did as it pleased with superb indifference to man. Its presence was constantly felt, and by slow degrees it became almost overwhelming. One finally had the impression that what the people did in the play mattered very little, whether they were good or bad, did the right or the wrong thing. What really counted was the tremendous personality of the desert wind. When the simoom rose, everything seemed to go black, and the little men and women on the stage became so insignificant as to be swallowed up by the howling element.

Michelet once wrote a description of a storm he had seen in October 1859, at the mouth of the Gironde. The house he lived in at the time was well within sight of the Atlantic Ocean, and for five days Michelet was unable to leave this house because of the fury of the wind. The shutters had to be closed tight; no door could be opened, and the writer lived by candlelight. He wrote — what else could he do? — and gave us what might be called a portrait of a storm[11] such as was never surpassed, even by Hugo, who practically turns into a storm himself when he tackles the subject, or by Conrad with his uncanny understanding of nature in a passion; at the end of five days Michelet was almost driven out of his mind by the ceaseless shrieking of the wind, and through the shutters he watched the sea with a feeling of hatred. And being a nineteenth-century writer, and a great poet, he apostrophized the elements, the tempest, the raging sea: 'What is it you want?' he asked. And the sea, in true nineteenth-century fashion, replies: 'Your death and universal death, the annihilation of earth and the return to chaos.' Well, that storm of 1859 is certainly a very grand character, and it is difficult to imagine what kind of person could possibly be pitted against it in a novel, unless it were a Titan.

The nearest approach to a storm in human events is obviously a war or a revolution, and if you introduce that kind of storm in a book, it is bound to work havoc with characters unless you can handle it with the masterful hand of a Tolstoy, but you will recall that Tolstoy was surnamed God the Father, with no blasphemous intent, by the Russians, and he could do pretty well as he chose. To fancy one can use war or a revolution simply as a background is a dangerous illusion. The background is apt to move forward, so to speak, and make the characters look puny — and funny. It is as if one used a number of grizzly bears as a background for a tea party. Sooner or later, there would be no tea party, there would be nothing but bears. That is exactly what happens in novels about wars and revolutions. The events devour the characters, or, as I have said, they become the real characters. When Zola wrote *La Débâcle*, he used the Franco-Prussian War of 1870 as his theme, but he knew what he was doing and he knew what was bound to happen. The war was the main personage of his book; as for the others, the human beings, men and women, although realistically observed and depicted with all the coarseness and brutality of the school to which Zola belonged, they have no inner reality; as individuals they seem futile; to use one of E.M. Forster's expressions, they are flat, not round, but they do exist as a crowd, they exist inasmuch as they are a part of the war.

It may be argued, however, that a book of this kind can hardly be called a novel. Indeed, I insist that it isn't. What it is, really, is an epic, a prose epic, as almost always happens when human characters in a book are in conflict not with each other but with a superhuman force. Thus we have epics of the sea, of the wind, of the cold or of events of very great magnitude which are apt to get beyond our control ...

Lectures on Novel Writing

These are some of the notes for lectures given at Goucher College, Maryland, from March 24 to May 18, 1941.

I

No books are to be used in connection with this course. There will be, of course, many references to famous novels, but the only writings we shall discuss will be yours.

Why? Because the danger of studying great models too closely is that it encourages whatever tendencies we may have to imitate, and the desire to imitate the great is almost irresistible in beginners. Imitation is not always as bad as Emerson said[12]. In art as well as in literature it has brought into existence an impressive number of masterpieces. Not always easy to detect, because the imitation sometimes surpasses the original, and the original is forgotten. Nevertheless it has done more harm than good.

I shall therefore ask you to try to forget that you have ever read a piece of fiction when you sit down to write. We must try to do something really creative, not imitative. We must try to find out what really belongs to us in the field of imagination. We must try to live by our own means, without borrowing from friends.

To write a novel is one of the most exciting experiences, because it teaches us more about ourselves than almost any mental form of activity. It makes us dig into our mind. You will be amazed to see how much there is in your mind, a world you may never have suspected, but, of course, this means very hard work, and you cannot expect to find anything that really belongs to you in your minds if you simply remember what other people have written.

Some writers are imitators but if they are great writers, they are great imitators, that is, they recreate their model, make it into something new, something better. Most writers, I am sorry to say, are poor imitators. They follow the fashion. If long books full of adventures are being read, they write long books full of adventures. And this goes on until, one day, a man decides to be himself and give the public something that really belongs to them.

Then this writer is acclaimed because he has written something highly original, instead of picking other authors' pockets, as it were. The public does not always realize where the originality of the book lies, but feels that it is being given real money instead of counterfeit notes.

So the first thing to bear in mind when you write a novel is that you want to be yourself. You don't want to be the echo of a bestseller. You want to speak with your own voice and express your own thoughts, not other people's thoughts.

It has been said that anyone could write at least one good book if he tried, that is, a book about himself. We do not know what we are capable of doing before we have really tried, and when we think we have really tried, as a rule, we have not even begun to try. Taine used to say that we must try to climb on our own shoulders.

The stuff good novels are made of is called life. But to transmute life into a novel is one of the most difficult things in the world, because if the operation is carried out by a clumsy person, life vanishes during the process and all that remains is a dead novel. How can this be avoided? By being absolutely sincere, by never writing what you feel is not true.

This is a very strange point. A real artist must speak the truth even when he is making up a story. How can a man speak the truth when he is writing fiction? By not saying anything which does not ring true.

Of course, when you are writing about yourself it is much easier to know what rings true and what does not. It is easy enough to tell other people lies, but it is impossible to tell oneself a lie and expect to be believed.

II

My intention is to tell you what I know about writing novels. If there were a receipt for writing a good novel, I would be only too glad to let you have it and to make use of it myself, but I don't know of any such receipt. I believe that you learn to write novels by writing novels, but I can give you certain hints which will save you trouble.

I expect to learn as much from you as you from me. This may seem strange, but you may find out someday that there is no better way of learning than to teach. And let no man think that he has nothing to learn (and no woman either). I expect to benefit by your mistakes, I also expect to be impressed and edified by your achievements!

A novel is a strange kind of dish, when you come to think of it, a sort of hodgepodge, with a great many ingredients in it. First of all, a narrative. As important as meat is to a stew. The author tells a story. Apart from the narrative proper, we have sometimes pages of dialogue which might belong to a play. Moreover, we are often treated to philosophical views enlarged upon at considerable length, or psychological analyses which sometimes retard the action, or descriptions written for description's sake that do not in any way help the narrative. The sauce is provided by the style, and if the sauce is bad, I am afraid the dish is spoiled.

III

My intention, as I told you yesterday, is to try to teach you what
I have learned myself in writing novels. I have asked you to
write a character sketch which will serve as a beginning for a
story. Having created a character, you will try to observe it, as
you would observe a real person in everyday life and see what
happens to it. I shall endeavor to tell you exactly how this is
done.

I cannot, of course, write your story for you, but I can guide
you. We must try to work together. I shall do everything I can
to throw light on your path, but you must remember that if you
do not make an effort, I can't very well help you. My task is to
try to awaken whatever talent you may have for telling a good
story. But first you must give me something concrete to work
on, something which you and I may use to build on. That is the
object of the character sketch you are going to give me. I could,
of course, deliver twenty or forty lectures on the different
methods of writing novels, and you might occasionally take
notes, but this wouldn't help you much. You might learn in an
abstract and theoretical sort of way how novels are written, but
unless you actually try to write one yourself, you will never
really know how this is done.

We shall now see how your character sketch is to be written.
You may have been a little puzzled, yesterday, when I told you
that I expected you to create a character, because it is one of the
most difficult things to do, but we can and we must try if we
want to learn how to write novels. The first thing to do is to
think. You mustn't begin to write and then think. You must
think first and think hard. What kind of person do I want as the
main character of my story? A man, a woman, a boy or a girl?
Can I form a mental picture of this person? Do I see him?

This last question is a very important one. When we think of someone we know well, we can form a mental picture of that person, and the more we think, the clearer the picture becomes. Not only do we remember the eyes, but the expression of the eyes; not only the shape of the features, but the impression they make on us, a pleasing or a disagreeable impression; and little by little, almost immediately in certain cases, the picture lives, we see the person we are thinking of. We see this person all the better if we have observed him carefully and if we have a good memory. So what you need in the case of a real human being is a good memory and certain powers of observation, that is, if you want to bring up a mental picture of him.

But what about a fictitious character, a person you are making up? How can we form a mental picture of a person we have never seen and who really does not exist? This is a little more difficult, but not so difficult as it may seem. Any one of us can almost immediately form a mental picture of a tall man with a white face and a black beard, or of a small, middle-aged woman with reddish hair, for instance, and a limp, or a child with blue eyes and a freckled nose. And the more we concentrate on this mental picture, the clearer it will become. And here a very curious thing will happen. Imagination will take the place of observation. You will observe this imaginary character as if it were a person you know, and this kind of observation is nothing but a form of imagination. The greater your imagination, the more vivid the mental picture. The better you see this mental picture, the more life you will put into it. A great artist is a man who sees the characters he is creating. He sees them with as much intensity as if they were walking and breathing in front of him. This is a sort of inner vision. His imagination is now his matter. Dickens, for instance, had this gift to such a point that he was able to make us see what he saw himself (Pip and the convict).

If you don't really see your characters, that is, if you have not sufficiently concentrated on what they look like, you will not be able to make your reader see them any better. If they live for you, they will live for your reader. To sum up what I have said, by seeing your characters, I mean forming a mental picture of them, a picture so clear, so intense, that in describing it, you will succeed in making your reader see almost exactly what you see yourself. And that is what people call talent. Talent is, among other things, the power to put into words a vivid mental picture.

Of course, imagination draws a great deal on observation. If you are in the habit of noticing people in real life, of observing how they dress and how they talk, what look comes into their eyes when they are pleased, or sad, or angry, it will be much easier for you to form a mental picture of a fictitious character. When you come to think of it, a fictitious character is a composite mental picture, that is, a mental picture made up of details observed in real life, some belonging to this person, some to that. We do this unconsciously. We think we are imagining when we are really remembering things and people we have seen and are putting them together to form a composite mental picture. For instance, if I imagine a tall man with a white face, a black beard, brown eyes and a hand with a scar, and if, by thinking of him for some time, I imagine that he is the kind of person that would wear a long black overcoat and shiny black overshoes, it may very well be that the black beard has been suggested to me by some real person's black beard, and the brown eyes by another real person's eyes; and the coat might belong to a third person, and I would assemble all these different elements and make one person of them, but the point I make is that the writer is not conscious of the process while he is forming his mental picture.

Of course, you will say: 'Why go to the trouble of making up a fictitious character when we can take a model from everyday life?' This can be done, of course, and is done by the very best writers, even though they themselves do not always realize it, but you will find that it is much more difficult to deal with a living person than with a fictitious character. You will make them do one thing in your story and they may surprise you in real life by doing something totally different because life is also a novelist, and the greatest of all novelists.

A very important point is the following: when you are making up your character, you will find it easier in the long run to imagine a person with whom you are in sympathy; I mean that you must be interested in your characters, you must feel sorry for them if something happens to them, you must try to be fond of them in spite of their faults. A lack of sympathy for his characters on the part of the author is a very grave fault.

If you are in sympathy with your characters, you may discover that when they talk they are expressing something you have felt or thought yourself. In a way, they are a part of yourself. If they are happy, it is your own happiness they are expressing; if they are disappointed, they are experiencing your own disappointments.

I need hardly tell you that the more you live, the greater your material will be, and you are all very young, but I feel sure you have something to say already.

You must be extremely careful in your choice of words. Words are like the little dabs of paint the painter uses to compose his picture. They must be just right. You don't have to use a great many to express what you mean. A good novelist can describe a man in five or six lines and have him standing in front of you, with his hat on his head and his cigar in his mouth. What you have to say, you must say as simply as possible. Remember that it is much more difficult to express oneself in a few words than in a great many. Try to sum up and to condense what you have to say and your writing will be much more forceful.

IV

Today I want to talk to you about the character or characters in relation to the plot. I have told you that if you have good, strong characters, the plot will take care of itself. What makes people act is willpower. Sometimes, of course, very weak people are driven to action by a very strong desire which takes the place of willpower. Anyway, if you take a group of people and put them into a book but deprive them of any kind of willpower or desire, you are going to have a very dull book on your hands, a book in which nothing can possibly happen. So your characters must have something in them that drives them to action unless they are made to act by outward circumstances. But the indispensable element in a novel is action.

How does action originate? You take the life of an ordinary human being, let us say the life of a stationmaster in a small town. He is moderately contented with things in general, he neither wonders whether he is happy or unhappy. He has enough to eat, he has friends, there is nothing remarkable about him, year in, year out, he goes about his business and nothing ever seems to happen to him. Not a very promising character. Yet we must see what we can make of him.

To begin with, what kind of person is he? What does he look like? You can imagine the kind of cap he wears, can you try to imagine the face beneath the cap? He would hardly be a shy man. It takes more than a shy man to stop a train. Indeed, stopping trains, being obeyed by such terrific animals as trains, may have given him an exaggerated idea of his own importance in this world, and there might be something slightly aggressive in his manner. Won't this show in his eyes, in his mouth, in his chin?

We must try to imagine what he is like, we must observe this fictitious character as if he were a living person standing in front of us. We must try to see in what respect he differs from all the stationmasters we have ever seen, having first tried to see in what respect he resembles the people of his profession. I mean that we must first present a typical stationmaster belonging to a very definite group of human beings. Then we must single him out of the group and characterize him in such a way that he cannot be confused with any one else.

Perhaps you think that he is too unromantic to make a good character, but novelists have learned from experience that apparently uninteresting people make first-rate material for stories. If you don't care for my stationmaster, you may choose a cook peeling potatoes and thinking over her worries. Perhaps she is an old woman with a good-for-nothing son who steals her money from her. Or perhaps she is a young cook somewhat overfond of a good time who is thinking of the ball she is going to that same evening. Or perhaps she is a pious cook who sings hymns. We had such a cook once, but she stole and we had to part with her.

This example I have chosen by way of showing you that you don't ever have to look very far for characters. In fact, one of the best characters you can possibly take is yourself. This does not mean that you have to write your novel in the first person, although great novels have been written in the first person with the author as the main character.

However, we are taking up the case of a character made up by the author, that is, a fictitious character with traits borrowed from this or that living person. And so we go back to the unpromising and unprepossessing stationmaster whose life seems a very uneventful one, but we must try to see it from his own point of view, we must try to imagine that we are the stationmaster, and if we can do that well, we are born novelists, and if we can't, we may be good philosophers, or essayists, but we are not novelists. A novelist is a man who can transform himself into the characters described in their book. Children can do this very well. They call it pretending. Let us pretend that we are soldiers, or kings ... Unfortunately, when children grow up they lose that gift, but when they are able to retain it and make use of it in novels, then, of course, they are hailed as great novelists, because talent is made up of things which most of us possessed in our childhood and almost all of us have lost in later years. You will often hear me refer to Dickens, because Dickens is one of the most typical novelists that ever lived, and one of the greatest creators of characters. The older you grow and the more you read him, the better you will realize that at heart he was a child and he saw the world very much as a child would see it, with the good on one side and the bad on the other, in sharp contrast. But he saw vividly, as a child does.

Well, you know how Dickens worked. He sat down at his desk every morning at nine and wrote until noon without stopping. Someone asked him how he made up his characters, and he said simply: 'By thinking of nothing else when I am at work.' That is, he didn't sit down and occasionally think of what he wanted to write, he didn't allow his mind to wander, he didn't pick up his watch and play with it, or draw faces on his blotting paper, he fixed his attention on Bill Sikes or Mrs. Jellyby and on nothing else until he actually *saw* them. This means very hard work. Talent is not a gift which allows one to work easily, talent is nothing if it is not accompanied by hard work.

Now, if you see your characters, they will act. You must watch them carefully until they begin to move, and get up and go about, and do things. You may be sure that our station-master, if he is a real person, is not simply going to blow a whistle and stop trains all day. He does that inasmuch as he belongs to a group of human beings called stationmasters. But we have seen that we must isolate him from all the other stationmasters in the world and discover what kind of man he is. He is probably an impatient person, apt to lose his temper when he plays cards with his friends. He may fuss with people, he probably expects everyone to mind every word he utters, to stop and go the way trains stop and go when he gives the proper signal. This is a sort of professional bent. I once heard a French bishop make an appeal for the refugees in a drawing room and he spoke very well, but I noticed that he had a strange way of repeating the last five or six words of each sentence. For instance, he said: 'The Russian refugees in Paris are now facing a very difficult problem, are now facing a very difficult problem.' When I asked someone why he did this, I was told that before being a bishop he had been a professor for many years at a Catholic university and that he had never been able to shake off the habit of repeating what he said because that was what he did when he dictated lessons to his students. And so, even in his purple robes, he was still a professor. In the same way, you may be sure that our stationmaster is a stationmaster at home and that he orders his wife about as he would a train. Can you imagine that she resents this? I suppose she does and here we have the beginning of some kind of action. The secret life of a stationmaster ...

V

Beware of set phrases. They are used by lazy writers who allow others to do their own thinking. Set phrases were good the first time they were used by the people who originated them, but now they are worn out. Try to coin your own phrases.

There are many things which a born novelist does almost unconsciously when he begins writing a novel. Nobody seems to have taught him those things. He knows them instinctively or he may have learned them from reading novels by other people. He knows, for instance, that the first thing to do is to secure his reader's attention by saying something of interest in the very first paragraph of his book. He can't afford to put it off, unless he happens to be a very well known author who already has the confidence of a fairly large reading public; he can't afford to be commonplace in the first page; in fact, it is very dangerous for him to be commonplace in any part of his book, but particularly so in the first page, because his reader won't stand it. A reader, as a rule, is a capricious person who insists on being entertained and absolutely refuses to be bored — I say 'a capricious person', because it is almost impossible to foresee what is going to amuse him and how long he will be interested in what we have to say. But you will find that he is much more kindly inclined to your author if the latter begins his book with something which strikes the imagination or appeals to the sense of humor. The other day I quoted the opening scene of *Great Expectations* with the escaped convict holding little Pip by the feet and shaking the pennies out of his pocket. This is a striking and picturesque scene which somehow whets your appetite and makes you want to go on with the book. Some of you may have read Tolstoy's book on his childhood and youth. They will no doubt recall that the book opens with the child Leon Nikolaievitch lying in bed and slowly being awakened by a funny noise; he opens his eyes and sees his French professor swatting flies on the wall just above the bed. And there is something so real and familiar about the scene that you don't forget it, and you are amused and interested, and you go on reading. A third example taken from modern literature, D.H. Lawrence's *The Plumed Serpent* begins with a bullfight which makes one of the main characters feel a little sick. Of course I hasten to say, there are some books that begin at a very slow pace and do not seem to have anything of great promise to offer, although they turn out to be very good later on, they are written, as a rule, by authors who are quite sure of their public, who know exactly how much their public will stand.

I believe that more men have it in them to write a book than is commonly thought. I don't say to write many books, but to write at least one, that is, a book about themselves. But it is hard to think of one's self as an interesting character. I don't mean that we are not interested in our own selves. I am afraid that we are more interested in ourselves than we are in any other person in the world, except under exceptional circumstances, but we are not usually inclined to think that we would make good characters in a novel. This is very often a fallacy, but it takes imagination to step out of ourselves, so to speak, and see what we are like in the eyes of other people. Also, it takes courage and deep regard for truth. To present an unflattering portrait of one's self is difficult, but it can be fascinating. 'What do you think of yourself?' is one of the most interesting questions that can be asked. Of course, it is an indiscreet question, but most of the most interesting questions that are asked are more or less indiscreet. Some years ago, a French writer said: 'There is no such thing as an indiscreet question, there are only indiscreet answers.' Be that as it may, the question, 'What do you think of yourself?' has been answered many times and very brilliantly by great writers of all countries. One of the most famous examples of this is Jean-Jacques Rousseau, who wrote, what he called his *Confessions*, but though he tried to be sincere, he did not always succeed. If ever you were to attempt anything of the kind, you would soon find out how difficult it is to be sincere even with the best intention in the world. We don't mind, under certain circumstances, we don't mind accusing ourselves of a very serious fault, but we don't want to appear mediocre, or stupid, and that is where sincerity is apt to break down. However, Rousseau's *Confessions* are not a novel. So let us take a novelist. Let us take Charlotte Brontë. Her first book, rejected by several publishers, was a novel called *The Professor*, and although the Professor is a man, many of his characteristic traits belong to the author of the book. But *The Professor* is only a sketch of a much longer book which Charlotte wrote many

years later: *Villette*. The principal character in *Villette* is Charlotte Brontë, just as the principal character in *Jane Eyre* is
Charlotte Brontë, and in neither book does she present a very
prepossessing likeness of herself. Of course, she does not say: 'I,
Charlotte Brontë.' She is writing a novel, she can write the
truth about herself and pass it off as fiction. That is what a great
many novelists do, more or less consciously, and they do it
because they are interested enough in their own personality to
see ...

VI

Those among you who have decided to abandon their novel
and to try their hand at a short story are missing a very good
opportunity to learn something of great importance, first about
the novel in general, secondly about themselves. You all know
how much even a slight knowledge of music will enhance our
pleasure in listening to a sonata or a concerto. Even to know
nothing more than the scales and to be able to decipher a simple
score will train our ear ever so little and enable it to enjoy music
a trifle more intelligently. In the same way, if you do try to
struggle with a novel and complete a few chapters, you will find
it much more interesting to read other people's novels than
before. You will be in a better position to appreciate the
author's intentions. You will have a better idea of how the book
is actually put together. It will strengthen your critical sense,
on the one hand, and compel you to develop your power of
concentration. How great a help this will prove to you in later
life I cannot begin to tell you.

Taine used to say that we should try to climb every day on

our own shoulders, that is, to try to develop mentally as much as possible. I am endeavoring to awaken in you something that is dormant. This something is in most of us. Willpower and concentration will bring it out. I do not say that you are all talented. Talent is a seemingly gratuitous gift, but talent without willpower is useless.

When we are very young, we are not aware of what goes on inside us, in our brain as well as in our heart. That is because we are fascinated by the outside world where everything seems new and exciting, but the day will come when we shall be more interested in the inside world, if I may say, the world which we carry in us, and we shall discover that it is far richer and more beautiful than anything our eyes can behold. When you are writing a book, you are compelled more or less to go into this interior world, because it is in this world that we get most of the material for our novels. Have you ever read a poem called 'The Mental Traveller?'[13] That is what we are when we write a book: mental travellers, and the country we travel in is, of course, as the name indicates, our minds.

In a previous lecture, I told you that even when you are writing a piece of fiction, you are really writing about yourself. When you describe a musician about to play his part in a symphony, or a gardener working in a garden, or any kind of man or woman whom you are imagining, you are actually writing about yourself as a musician, or a gardener, or any other so-called fictitious character. Fiction is a very misleading term. It seems to imply that what you are writing is untrue, is not according to fact. But fiction is, or should be, made of flesh and blood. When you write about a musician who is feeling a little nervous because he knows that in a minute or two the attention of the whole theater is going to concentrate on his performance, you must not think: 'I am describing a young musician', you must think: 'I am myself that musician and I am feeling nervous, because I am a little timid and afraid that everything is not going to go as smoothly as I wish.' Then, if you are really in earnest and concentrate sufficiently, you will become the character you describe and his emotions will be your own emotions. It is amazing how much we are able to do in that line.

Some of you may have read Flaubert's letters. On one occasion he tells how, in describing a nervous fit experienced by Mme Bovary, he became so intensely absorbed in his subject that he almost had a fit himself. The result is that when you read Flaubert's account of the fit you are almost appalled by the picture he gives of it; it is so real, so intensely real, not real simply from the scientific point of view, but real from the inside.

That is what truth does to you when you encounter it in a story or, for that matter, anywhere: it gives you a sort of shock. In the field of literature, this shock is decidedly a pleasant one; it creates a feeling of admiration in the heart of the reader. But that kind of truth does not only depend on the accuracy of observation, although observation is extremely important; it depends on how real and how deep the emotion is which you try to put into words. Even if your words are clumsy and you don't know very well how to work out your story, your description or your dialogue, if your feelings are real, if you are sincere with yourself, something will come out and show in what you write.

This question of sincerity is so important in writing a novel that you can hardly overestimate — I do not say its moral value — but its artistic value. You must write with your heart, with all your heart, if you want to produce a real novel. Your mind won't help you much if your heart is silent. I know what words are made of, what they hide and what they reveal. I know when they are trying to say something real and when they are simply there on a page in a perfunctory sort of way. Then, do not describe what you do not feel, do not say what you do not believe, above all do not pretend that you see what you are not seeing at all for lack of concentration. Remember that an author can be telling a lie when he describes the dress of a person who has never existed except in his imagination.

VII

As a matter of fact, not very many books begin with a description of the main character. It would seem a little too obvious, somehow. Novelists, as a rule, take pride in their subtlety, and to a great number of them, the way they approach a subject shows just how subtle they can be. Sometimes this approach is so devious that the reader is completely puzzled; he feels he is being led round and round in a maze. The other day we read a story by Virginia Woolf and in the middle of it the reader stopped and asked what the story was about. Of course, that is Mrs. Woolf's way and it goes with her talent. By contrast, how very simply an artist like Tolstoy begins his stories. His approach to a subject is almost childlike. He starts out by telling you that So-and-So, his main character, is unhappy because his conscience hurts him, for instance. And you are almost shocked by this complete absence of artfulness. Of course, this artlessness is only apparent. It takes a very great artist to be artless in the way Tolstoy was. The secret of his appeal to so many thousands of readers is that he believed what he said and he saw what he described.

You know that his theory was that great artists should write their books for the people, which explains the almost Bible-like simplicity of his style in his later books and also that directness of approach which I have mentioned. How much truth there is in his theory as to the necessity of writing, or painting, or composing music for the people, I shall not discuss here, because this is not a lecture on Tolstoy, but I can't help thinking that Beethoven's later quartets were not composed for the purpose of entertaining grocers, nor did Meredith write for mechanics.

To see ... to a novelist, this is certainly one of the most important problems to be dealt with, and in my estimation, novelists can be classed in two general categories: those who see what they are writing about, and those who don't, and I needn't tell you which category I prefer.

Of course, to be able to form a mental image is in itself a gift, and not a very common one. A few days ago in a conversation between friends, for some reason the problem of thinking without words was brought up. Can one think without words? Is it possible to think in images? When a painter thinks of blue, does he form a mental picture of that color, or does he think the word *blue*, or does he do both at the same time? Well, it is a fascinating problem, because apparently no satisfactory answer can be given. A lady said that she was incapable of thinking of a cat without immediately writing c-a-t in her mind, but she teaches languages and her mind is permeated with words as is the mind of almost every philologist. She told us about a man whose mind is of a very different type 'This man,' she said, 'actually sees what he reads, or talks about.' For instance, he told the lady, 'If someone mentions a dog, I immediately see that animal.' 'Where?' asked the lady. The man waved his hand vaguely: 'Oh, out there, in front of me.' 'But doesn't he get in the way?' 'Oh no,' was the reply. 'He's transparent.'

Well, we all laughed, but I couldn't help thinking that this man's answer was very interesting and that, if it was really sincere, many novelists might envy this gift for visualizing.

The power to visualize is one of those many gifts which education takes away from us. It might be said, in a very general sort of way, that education teaches us to cope with ideas. Education is not simply information; education teaches us how to use our minds. But there is a price to pay, and the price seems to be the loss of several gifts that were ours as children. Critical sense, that is the power to judge, to distinguish, is acquired very often at the expense of imagination.

As a rule, children visualize much better than grown-ups, and imagination is nothing but the power to visualize. In the same way, some races who are nearer the state of childhood visualize better than the more intellectually developed branches of the human family. Arabs, for instance, see with an intensity that is quite foreign to us.

In Morocco they still have public storytellers, as they did centuries ago in Europe. These men stand in the market square and begin telling a story, people gather around them, usually squatting on their heels and listening very intently while these ageless tales are repeated with variations. What the tales are like you can imagine if you are familiar with the *Arabian Nights*. I must add, however, to be truthful, that they thoroughly enjoy American stories. One of their favorite characters is Nick Carter. How they ever got hold of Nick Carter is still a little mysterious; I suppose it was through the moving pictures. Moving pictures, by the way, are very popular among the people of North Africa, but they are shown in a peculiar way. Bits of film are pieced together in a haphazard sort of way, with no idea of continuity. If they make sense, all the better. If they don't, they are still wildly appreciated. Well, to go back to the storytellers, what is interesting to us is the way the audience reacts to the stories. If something unfortunate happens to the hero, the audience groans and beats its breast. Fists are clenched and cries of rage are uttered when the villain appears. So much excitement is caused at times that the story has to be cut short. All of which would tend to prove that these people *see* what is being described to them.

A good novelist, a great novelist, is in many respects a child. Dickens, whom I am always quoting as a typical novelist, and certainly one of the very greatest in any language, Dickens was a child with the experience of a man. A genius, I mean a creative, literary genius, is often a man who has succeeded in retaining the imagination of childhood.

As I Look Back

Originally written in French in 1941 in Baltimore and immediately translated into English by the author.

As I look back on the period which came so dramatically to its close in the month of June 1940, I realize that I am now in a better position to understand it than I was twelve months ago. Time is a marvelous interpreter. Let a few weeks go by, and the hidden meaning of our present experiences will suddenly appear. What seemed uninteresting and trivial at the moment may some day take on great importance; even the drabbest of hours will count and in time occasion longing. I have experienced boredom in the Paris of my twenties; would that I could recapture those minutes of ennui! I could somehow change them into something like happiness today.

One of the many little quarrels I had with life when I first began to write was that I had been born out of time. There was, I thought, something wrong with the year of my birth. I regretted not having come into this world at the beginning of a long and brilliant literary period, such as the Age of Elizabeth or the French Nineteenth Century (roughly between 1830 and 1870). In my mind — I was then twenty-two or three — there was nothing great about our modern living writers except their pretensions. Marcel Proust had died a few months before, in an ugly little street near the Trocadéro, and there seemed to be no one of his importance to take his place at the head of French writers. I was extremely severe. I looked around, turned down one author after another, and quickly decided that I had come in for a very dull moment in French Literature.

This error was due, partly, to what I might call an optical delusion. I failed to grasp the picturesqueness of the period in which I lived because I did not try to see it through the eyes of future generations, as we should always do if we wish to have a more or less correct view of our own times. I looked back hungrily at the days when writers wore red velvet waistcoats and wrote flamboyant verse. It did not occur to me that, had I lived at a time when a red velvet waistcoat was the thing to wear, I should probably have sighed for the age of periwigs and lace jabots, and in the age of periwigs I might conceivably have longed for Montaigne's ruff, and so forth down through the Dark Ages, until my superstitious nostalgia for the past carried me back to the good old days of cuneiform brick tablets. But I was young and had strange notions about things. I considered that I lived in a colorless literary period, that authors wore colorless clothes and wrote in a colorless way. Or if they weren't colorless and dressed or wrote in a flashy style, they belonged to that crowd of shabby amateurs, the Montparnos[14], who misused the most beautiful language in the world and went about in slippers that would have disgraced an 'apache', allowing their hair to grow long and flaunting outrageous striped shirts with collars wide open. Their audacities irked me. I particularly disliked their mania for turning out poems with verbs, articles, prepositions and conjunctions left out, with showy adjectives forcibly harnessed to reluctant nouns, giving the impression that instead of poetry we were reading telegrams written by lunatics.

In a way, I was right. There were two currents in modern French literature: one wild, the other, apparently, tame and well behaved but a trifle dull at first glance or, let us say, a little serious. This is more or less in the French tradition of the 1820s when the Neo-Classics and the early Romanticists were beginning to affront each other, but alas, there was little promise of 1830 in the air.

After the turmoil created by Proust's magnificent achievement, there was a lull in the world of letters and a curious feeling of hesitancy. The great invalid had overshadowed everything from his sickroom of the rue Hamelin, but now he was in his grave and a hush ensued. The oak had been felled and the shrubs that had grown at its base reared their heads in the sun and wondered why they too shouldn't grow up into nice big trees, and to be sure some did.

Proust died in November 1923. He had lived just long enough to catch the first glimpse of his literary glory, that glory which Balzac said was the sun that sheds its light on the dead. Now people no longer called him Proust, they called him Marcel, a sure sign, in Paris, that supreme literary success had been achieved. Everybody had known him, more people perhaps than he himself suspected. Everybody had some anecdote to relate about Marcel's eccentricities, Marcel's prodigious memory, Marcel's celebrated '*gentillesse*', Marcel's generosity, or Marcel's infernal cruelty, for the portrait was a composite one and one got the impression, from so many conflicting reports, that the model must have been even more strangely and deeply complicated than his books led one to believe. He was himself the most abstruse of Marcel Proust's characters. Much ado was made after his death about the keys to his characters, but although each of his friends claimed to have the one and only key to his own character, it is a noteworthy fact that none of these ingenious instruments seemed to fit the lock, and thus it is that this man who expressed himself most abundantly on what he felt and thought remains almost as mysterious as if the had held his peace.

Paris is certainly one of the most gossipy cities in the world and many stories were circulated about this extraordinary man, neither was it always very easy to trace them back to their origin. Some were rather absurd, like the one about Proust putting out rats' eyes with a pin; they were interesting in a way, because they harked back to the days of Count de Montesquiou[15], one of the most picturesque characters of the late nineteenth century and certainly one of Proust's models. Personally, I think that Marcel Proust was far too busy writing his books to put out rats' eyes, a frivolous and disgusting occupation when well considered.

Among the authenticated stories about Proust, there are two or three which I thought amusing to pick out, because they show him in different lights. Probably one of his most amiable traits was his exquisite politeness. It hid what politeness so often hides: boredom, contempt and the milder forms of animosity, but it ingratiated him to many and in some instances he bordered on genuine charity. A friend of his left us an account of a small dinner party which he gave at the Ritz, where Marcel Proust was often to be seen whenever his asthma allowed him to leave his room. One of the people he had invited that evening was an old gentleman whom we will call the Marquis of N., a most unprepossessing person, the butt of many unkind jokes because he had been abandoned by his wife. He was a semi-invalid and suffered from a nervous disease which compelled him to walk sideways and to throw himself on a chair instead of sitting down quietly like every one else. I may add that he was considered one of the worst bores in existence and that he was, for that reason, sedulously avoided by all. However, as soon as this unfortunate man appeared in the dining room of the Ritz, Marcel Proust managed to guide him to his chair in such a way that his guest's sinister and involuntary antics were not noticed. Nor did our author's kindness stop there: all during that meal, he contrived to ask the Marquis the very questions which the old gentleman could answer in an interesting way; in one word, he brought him into existence again, so that instead of a decrepit human being brought low by pleasure and gambling, the other guests beheld and listened to what one of them calls a man of great aristocracy and much wit. Such was the miracle performed by genius allied to the most delicate form of charity, I mean '*gentillesse.*'

Now let us play the part of the devil's advocate and show Marcel Proust in one of his more fiendish moods. However, the story I am about to relate needs something of a preface. It was told me by one of his friends and warmest admirers and I cannot, of course, vouch for its absolute authenticity in as much as I did not witness the incident, but you have read Marcel Proust's novels and you know enough about the man to tell whether this story rings true or not. Many years ago, at the very dawn of this lovely century, there lived in Paris a musician whose work was then extremely popular. In fact, his music had much to recommend it to the ears of many, being sweet, tuneful and a trifle sentimental. Among those who were most delighted by these easy strains was Marcel Proust, and he said so; he even wrote about it; but the years went by and the fashion changed, and it became no longer the thing to like this pretty music of 1900, and Proust, who was ever a slave to fashion, remembered what he had said and written on the subject, felt considerably annoyed and even grew a little resentful. It is somewhat provoking to find out one has admired the wrong thing, particularly when this admiration has been publicly expressed. Meanwhile the poor musician had fallen on rather evil days and was in need of financial help. Proust knew this and no doubt wished to be kind, but the very presence of this unfortunate artist was a source of humiliation to him because it reminded him of what he now considered one of his worst errors of judgment. Well, it happened one evening that the musician and the novelist met in the company of several well-known writers whom Marcel Proust was naturally enough anxious to impress. I may add that Proust and the musician[16] had been friends for many years and you can imagine what an awkward situation arose between these two men, each one knowing exactly what the other thought. There was an embarrassed silence, then Proust, in a voice already full of those celebrated hesitations which somehow found their way into the man's style, began with studied tactfulness to bemoan the fate of those who have experienced disfavor after having had a taste of glory. With an exquisite choice of words and endless circum- locutions, he then hinted that it was a duty and an honor to help an artist in distress, and finally, not without apologizing profusely for what he was about to do and begging everybody's pardon with imploring looks, offered his old friend to take him on as his secretary, but, he added, 'you must understand that I am not very wealthy and that I could not give you as much as I would like to.' He then named a sum so very moderate that it seemed little short of an insult. This offer was icily rejected by the musician whose face blanched with suppressed rage; whereupon Marcel Proust showed every sign of being most dreadfully grieved and mortified, not quite succeeding, however, in convincing all those present that his distress of mind was absolutely sincere. It was not very long before the story began to go the customary rounds in the Paris drawing rooms and was generally interpreted as a very Proust-like revenge on 1900.

One of his friends has an interesting story to tell about Proust's almost uncanny power of observation. It was said that he had an eye as perfect as that of a fly, which I understand is one of the greatest wonders of nature. His eye seemed to take in everything at once and on all sides. Shortly after the First World War, *Anthony and Cleopatra* was given at the Paris Opera by a particularly brilliant company. Every one of any note in the literary and artistic world was invited and, of course, Marcel Proust, whose fame was already very great. The occasion was far too important a one to miss, so he left his stuffy little room and, wrapped in furs and flannel, dragged himself to the Opera and sat in the back part of a box from which seat he could only with difficulty get a glimpse of the stage. This did not seem to bother him very much. He leaned over and, during the whole play, talked in a low murmur to the ladies who sat in front of him; neither did he stop during intermissions. Shakespeare halted for a rest, but not Proust; he went straight on. All this much to the annoyance of his friends who had accompanied him and could not understand why he paid so little attention to the play. A few days later they saw him again and one of them reproached him for having been so inattentive at the Opera. Whereupon Marcel Proust's eyes began to sparkle as they did whenever anything amused him and he raised his hands in mock indignation. He then embarked on a long and brilliant monologue in which almost everything connected with that evening was described and thoroughly discussed: the play itself and Mme Rubinstein's acting; a certain intonation in the voice of M. de Max, who took the part of Anthony; the peculiar lighting of the stage during the banquet scene; several things that had been said in the box next to the one in which Proust sat, not to mention a few minor incidents which had occurred among the spectators. On and on did he talk until his friends, amazed and perplexed, were forced to come to the co..clusion that Marcel Proust must have sat, that evening, in almost every seat in the house and noted everything with the most scrupulous and indefatigable attention.

When this extraordinary man died, there was, as I have hinted before, a certain feeling that somehow a world had disappeared with him, a sort of Atlantis which could not be conjured up again. Nevertheless, this did not prevent the French publishers from printing new books; in fact, seldom did they ever print as many books as they did in the years following Proust's death. It was a period of literary inflation. Every week saw the birth of a new author who was immediately proclaimed a genius by his publishers. One got the impression that Paris was full of young men with a university degree in one pocket and a contract with a publisher in the other, but upon reading their lucubrations, it became clear that more often than not the degree was missing. Glance at any French publisher's list between 1923 and 1930 and you will be amazed to see how many names have sunk into permanent oblivion; they fluttered for a few days on the lips of a bewildered and well-meaning public that tried desperately to keep up with modern literature, but they soon perished from the memory of humanity. The trouble was that those young writers did not exist in themselves; they were at most mere reflections of their more talented elders. Among the latter, two stood out with particular glamor: Jean Giraudoux and Paul Morand. Although these writers differed in almost every conceivable way, their names were nevertheless coupled, because they represented new tendencies in French literature (or were thought to by the general public) and represented them with considerable bril-

liance. If I were writing a literary history of the last decades in
France, I would try to show that Giraudoux, who appeared so
modern and so bold to the readers of 1925, was really in the
tradition of the 1600s, a direct descendant of the Précieux and a
not very distant cousin of Euphues[17]. He had mastered the art of
saying things in a delicate and unexpected way which took one
by surprise and created pleasurable impressions. His exquisite
irony was tempered by a sense of what is poetical in life; he was
too self-conscious to be a real poet, however, and too skeptical
of humanity to write seriously about it, but he expressed
himself with inimitable grace and the way he said things
seemed somehow more important than the things themselves.
At times he was so clever and elliptical that his reader was left a
little puzzled, yet each sentence was as transparent as crystal.
Never have I felt so heavy or so stupid as once when, having
read fifteen or twenty pages of one of Giraudoux's early novels,
I realized that I had not the faintest idea what the story was
about, but I was completely dazzled by the style and quite
willing to confess myself a lout and a Philistine. I was then
about twenty. A few years later I met Giraudoux. He and I
happened to belong to the same literary committee for a prize
awarded to the best novel written within the year by an
unknown beginner. He was a trifle taller than I, thin, well
dressed in sober grays, and wore very large rimmed spectacles
through which he looked at the outer world with an amused
expression. What seemed to me most noticeable about him was
his obvious desire not to be in any way noticeable. He was clean
shaven and spoke, to my surprise, in the most direct manner;
there was not the slightest trace of affectation in this man whose
style was nothing but a mass of delightful mannerisms. Far
from conforming to the conventional idea of the rather untidy
and epigrammatic writer, he put one in mind of a business man,
neat in his dress and matter of fact in his speech. When asked to
give his opinion of some of the manuscripts he had read, he
talked in a precise and dispassionate way, as he might have

talked about the stock market. Most surprising to me were the favorable judgments he passed on what I deemed insipid and sentimental trash. I remember hearing him defend, in a totally impassive voice, a vilely written and most commonplace love story which had been submitted to us, and when I protested on the ground that it was a dull piece of work, he looked at me with an expression of very mild surprise, as if to say: 'What on earth does it matter? Why all this flurry about a book?' He seemed to refuse to take anything too seriously, either his own work or the work of others. He was the kind of man who, if he were to quote the Bible, would quote Ecclesiastes, with a smile. I must have seemed awfully foreign to him, but I liked him and admired him. Years, many years, went by and we saw little of each other. Then the war broke out while I was in this country and I went back to Paris. My first visit was to Jean Giraudoux, who had been named minister of propaganda[18]. He hadn't changed in the least; he was still as courteous and impassive as before, and he smiled. I told him that the friends of France in America complained that all the propaganda was made by the Germans and none by the French. He listened with great politeness, as he had listened years before to my grievances against a tiresome love story, and all of a sudden I realized, with a pang in my heart, that I was being foreign again and that my words were not heeded. After a few minutes' conversation, he took me to the door and said that I could do nothing more for France than to go on writing books. The words were kindly spoken and, coming from such a writer, should have pleased me, but as the door closed behind me, I had to struggle against a sudden feeling of distress, a sudden foreboding that things were going wrong in France, and above all, that Euphues was no match for Propaganda Minister Goebbels.

Paul Morand, whom I also met in the early twenties, was as unpretentious as Giraudoux and just as '*effacé*', in spite of his extraordinary success. The sure mark of success is imitation, and no one was quite so widely and slavishly imitated in France as Morand, particularly among the young who adopted his telegraphic style with frenzied enthusiasm but lacked his ability in handling this difficult and ungrateful medium. Like many other writers of talent, Morand was responsible for large quantities of bad writing in which his own style was reflected as a man's face is reflected in a convex or concave mirror. With an eye for colorful details and a gift for lightning brevity in expressing himself, he gave the reading public a jolt with his first book of tales: *Ouvert la Nuit.* Today, when we reread the book, it seems difficult to realize what shocked the reader of 1920 when confronted with this violent form of literature, because it has lost much of its violence and the element of surprise has almost entirely gone from it. Authors like Faulkner and Dreiser appear far more brutal and audacious, but we must not forget that in 1920 the reign of Anatole France and his well-oiled sentences had only just come to a close, and serious, heavy, psychological old Bourget with his nineteenth-century ideas was still very much read; in fact, both France and Bourget were living when Morand began heaving verbs overboard and trampling syntax underfoot. The period after the war was marked by a general assault on grammar as well as on conventional morals in a vigorous reaction against the hated bourgeois spirit. It was really a revolt of the schoolboy against his teachers or, if you prefer, of the child against his parents, as Freud might have said, and Freud had much to do with it. Morand played a conspicuous part in this crusade against respectability, but the wonder of it was that, of all Frenchmen one might meet in Paris, he was among the most conventional in looks and manner. He was medium height and inclined to be a little stocky, with a yellowish complexion and black, intelligent eyes in a chubby face. He spoke in a quiet voice with apparently no desire to shock or dazzle; like almost every French writer, he had stories to tell, and he told them well, that is, briefly, but he was

anything but a talker or a wit; he listened with exemplary
politeness and his head a little on one side, ever ready to smile
at a joke and rejoin with another joke; an average, well-bred
Frenchman, but not one to draw circles of delighted listeners
around him like Cocteau, rather one of those listeners himself,
and as attentive and observant a listener as ever breathed on
the banks of the Seine. There are thousands of stories about
Cocteau, who is one of the most picturesque characters of this
period, as I hope to show in a little while; there are stories about
Gide and a few about Mauriac, because, as a rule, a good writer
sooner or later ends by building up a legend about himself, but
Giraudoux and Morand do not seem to have bothered about
this. I can think of no anecdote about Morand except, perhaps,
one which he tells himself in about fifteen or twenty words.
Very early in his career, before he had come to know the
meaning of the word success, he went to consult a palmist, as
the cleverest among us will do occasionally. She gave his hands
one look and said: 'Sorry. You have no fate line.' Now 'fate
line', in French, is called *ligne de chance*, which can mean 'fate
line' or 'line of luck.' 'No "*ligne de chance*"', said Morand. 'Very
well, I'll make one.' Whereupon he seized a knife and made
one, long and deep.

Morand's books were published by the *Nouvelle Revue Française*, generally known as the NRF. The NRF (later owned by
Gallimard) had a very long list of authors, good, bad and
indifferent, and somewhere at the top of the list was André
Gide, and the reason why I say somewhere at the top of the list
is that the names of Marcel Proust and Paul Claudel were to be
found in the same region, but as time went on and the flurry
caused by Marcel Proust had subsided, it became clear that not
only did Gide head the list of the NRF, but he *was* the NRF. The
NRF printed books of all sorts by authors who, for the most
part, had very little in common, and yet as books kept pouring
out in endless flow from the little house in the old rue de
Grenelle, it finally came to be recognized that there was such a

thing as what was called '*un ton NRF*' meaning a certain attitude of mind and a way of expressing oneself which distinctly belonged to number three, rue de Grenelle. The accusation was preferred against the NRF that it was producing something which its adversaries called chapel literature, by which they meant, not, of course, religiously minded books, but books written for a small public of initiates, or, as the literary jargon of the day had it, for a 'chapel'. Not all the books printed had this character, indeed most of them didn't, but those that really counted seemed to partake of that NRF spirit and were slowly monopolizing, or trying to monopolize, modern French literature.

It would take a very long time to prove or disprove that statement. Let us see, first of all, what this famous '*ton NRF*' consisted of. If I had to sum it up in one word, I might use the word *seriousness*. If I had to name one of the principal dogmas of this chapel, I should probably speak of its fanatical passion for sincerity. Now, the French have always loved sincerity; moreover, it is my firm belief that they are among the most serious people in this world, in spite of their reputation for frivolousness. After all, they produced Calvin, and Descartes, and Pascal, and Port-Royal, to say nothing of the leaders of the Revolution. Nevertheless, and here a clear distinction must be made, it is quite true that they love laughter. Any student of Rabelais will tell you that no man was ever more serious, at heart, than the author of *Gargantua*; he was as serious as any reformer, in spirit, but he loved laughter. The same is true of Voltaire, who was indeed earnest in spite of his perpetual grin. Seriousness has always appealed to the French but they have always avoided the mistake of confusing seriousness with a long face. And this is precisely what some writers had against the most typical of the NRF authors: they said they pulled long faces.

It wasn't their seriousness that they held against these NRF gentlemen, it was the fact that they had long faces, because long faces are un-French. And this brings us to a very interesting point and a very delicate one, too: during the long war between French Protestantism and the French kings, it was contended by the latter that Protestants were dangerous because they formed 'a state within the state.' They weren't like the rest of the nation, their ways were strange to Catholic France, and for that reason, among others, they were ruthlessly persecuted and finally driven out of the land. Now, it is a strange fact that French Protestants have to this very day kept certain characteristics which differentiate them from the majority of Frenchmen. They themselves, let me hasten to say, are excellent Frenchmen: they are hard-working, serious, oh very serious, charitable and courageous, and France is greatly indebted to them; in fact, no better citizen can be found than a good French Protestant, but as I have hinted before, he is apt to be a little grave, he is apt not to see the point of a joke, or he may disapprove of it. And there is nothing to be done about it: once a Protestant, always a Protestant, or, as Henry IV put it after his conversion to Catholicism: 'The herring cask always smells of herring.'

It may seem a far cry from Henry of Navarre to the NRF, but you will presently see what I am driving at. By slow degrees, André Gide had come to the very fore of French Literature and critics were beginning to say that he was monopolizing the NRF. He denied this repeatedly, but his adversaries were just as dogged as he was. Now, Gide is a Protestant. He is a Protestant to the core, although, by birth, he is half Catholic. There are many ways of being a Protestant. You can be a Protestant and not believe in Protestantism; I mean that there is such a thing as a Protestant cast of thought which does not necessarily imply an adherence to a religious creed. A Protestant can drift away from the beliefs of his youth and still be a Protestant in his general attitude towards life, in his manner of speech, in his ways, and this is particularly true of French Protestants, who still retain the fighting spirit of

minorities and that obstinacy which was so maddening to
Cardinal de Richelieu.

I wonder what Gide would say if he could hear me call him a
Protestant. He would probably shake his head and clear his
throat, as he did when he was a little embarrassed, and mumble
that the epithet is not unsuitable, if properly qualified; one day
in 1930 or 32, we were talking about this very thing, about
Protestantism. He had been nettled, a few days before, by an
attack from one of his oldest and most disloyal enemies, and
referred with great bitterness to his adversary's distortion of
truth. All of a sudden something flared in his black eyes, and he
exclaimed: 'Only Protestants have a real regard for truth: they
have given the world its greatest scientists, its greatest his-
torians, its boldest explorers!' He continued in this vein for a
few seconds, absolutely motionless except for an occasional and
indignant shake of the head, and I could not help thinking, in
spite of the flagrant unfairness of his words: 'What a fine
explosion.'

The first time I met him, in 1923, he wore under his coat a
black sweater, the sleeves of which covered his wrists and a part
of his hands. We were having tea at a friend's house, the friend
being Jacques de Lacretelle, a novelist who since has become
an Academician and is, by the way, a Protestant. What struck
me most the first time I ever looked at Gide was his eyes. I don't
think I have ever seen any with quite that look of fixed
attention, the look of a man who will not allow his thoughts to
wander but sternly and ceaselessly brings them back to one
point; it was a look of almost uncanny penetration which lent
great intellectual beauty to the thin, narrow face; the forehead
was high and dome-shaped, like that of Shakespeare or Lenin;
when he smiled, which he did once or twice, with a slight effort,
he showed a row of glistening white teeth. He struck me as
being rather taller than the average and wore a tweed suit. I
don't remember what he said, but one thing impressed me very
deeply, nor have I ever been compelled to revise this first

impression: his extraordinary youthfulness. The moment he spoke, one completely forgot that he was fifty-three or four: his manner of speech, his points of view, all had the freshness and spontaneity of a young man. There was even a certain shyness about him, which at first I took for a piece of affectation. He listened admirably, spoke little and diffidently, and only once in a while stressed a word as only a very careful writer will do in ordinary conversation. At the end of thirty minutes or so, he got up, wrapped himself in a long cape made of dark gray wool, the kind shepherds wear in France, put on a rather funny little tweed hat and bid us good-bye.

'Did you notice the black sweater?' asked Lacretelle when he had gone. 'His enemies would call that a Protestant touch, I suppose.'

And he asked me what I thought of him. I was apt to be very flippant in those days. I said that he looked like Satan disguised as a tourist. It wasn't a very polite thing to say, but there was as much truth in it as there is in certain caricatures of well-known people. Nor do I think that Gide would have minded this description of his appearance; indeed, I rather fancy it might have flattered him.

We had lunch together, two years later, when I had written my first novel and he had expressed the desire to see me. I then had occasion to notice that his shyness was not affected, as I first imagined. Incredible though it may seem, it took little to send color to his cheeks. There was something baffling about the mental fortifications which he threw up all around him when anything like a personal matter was even distantly hinted at. Yet here was the man who was now being hailed as the greatest living master of French prose. Successful writers are not always so reserved. Later we came to know each other a little better and a friendship developed of which I am very proud. Here, however, I must clear up a slight misunderstanding which might well result from a casual reading of my diary. André Gide is often mentioned in my diary, usually at some

length, and the impression might be conveyed by these entries
that I saw him often, whereas, in point of fact, we saw each
other rather seldom, but when we did we almost always
decided to make a day of it, lunching or dining together and
then trudging through the streets in endless conversation,
telling each other of things we had seen or read in the past
months and confiding literary plans of all descriptions. Gide is
the most indefatigable walker, and I have often thought that it
was curiosity that prevented him from feeling tired as we
strolled from one end of Paris to the other: his attention was
always on the alert for something of interest to observe and little
escaped him that was worthy of notice, an odd face, or a
strangely worded sign or stray bits of conversation from pas-
sersby, the latter being quite often a source of merriment or
surprise. To give an adequate idea of Gide's conversation, I can
only say that it is immensely varied without ever being trivial or
futile. What he says is always worth saying and often worth
recording, not only because of its intrinsic value but also
because of the singular and felicitous way in which it is
expressed. He speaks well-nigh as carefully as he writes, with
that unexpected turn of phrase which has marked him out as
one of the makers of his own language. The characteristic of a
great language is that it is perpetually in the making, I mean
that it is perpetually becoming something different although,
fundamentally, it remains the same. This change is brought
about partly by the people, by the man in the street in his
everyday speech, partly by great writers who influence style
and modify the language to such an extent that it becomes
almost impossible to write, after they are gone, as one might
have written before they appeared. In a way, they might be
called the creators of the language. A few minutes' talk with
Gide would suffice, I believe, to show an open-minded and
well-educated person that he is not only a careful writer but one
of those creators I have mentioned. There is the French spoken
by everyone else and there is the French spoken by him: it is

essentially French, but it is essentially Gide's French. If it were taken down in short-hand and studied, as it well deserves, I think that what would strike the student more than anything else, is the paucity of words used; yet these words, though few in number, are used with such exquisite preciseness that the whole effect is one of richness and variety. I remember a story about Baudelaire who gave a copy of his *Flowers of Evil* to an Academician and was rewarded, a few days later, with the following question: 'Don't you know, M. Baudelaire, that certain words should never be coupled?' Now what was true of Baudelaire is true to a lesser degree of André Gide: he couples words which are not usually coupled, and he couples them in such a way that, although they are simple and commonplace enough, they create an impression of freshness and novelty and stimulate the imagination. For that reason it is really delightful to hear André Gide tell a story: he is careful not to make it long and each word is so admirably chosen and placed that one wonders whether he has not actually rehearsed the whole performance.

I have spoken of him as a shy man, as I still believe he is. The first evening we ever spent together, in the summer of 1928, is referred to in Gide's diary. We have often laughed about it since. I was then at least as reserved as he was and wracked my brain in an effort to find something to say which would neither be indiscreet, nor commonplace. To praise an author's work to his face seemed to me almost rude in those days. To speak of my own work would have been, I feared, ridiculous. And, of course, any allusion to my own personal way of living, or Gide's, would have brought a blush of horror to my face. Moreover, I had read very little of what he had written, knew practically nothing of what he thought or what he liked. We had dinner at the Traktir's[19], a strange place for Gide to be in, not one he liked at all, and when dinner was over, we walked to the Champs-Élysées and finally found our way to a place called the Lido, a large subterranean café made dazzling with lights and mirrors.

There was an orchestra on a stage and a rather large pool of water in the middle of the café; towards eleven, a man in evening dress announced the great attraction of the evening was about to begin, namely, *Une Nuit à Venise*. Whereupon a gondola was produced and set afloat in the pool, and in the gondola sat a lady in a black domino; she sang Offenbach's 'Barcarolle' and made night hideous with her yowls. I did not feel very happy. There was too much noise, too much light, too much of everything I loathed here, and I knew perfectly well that Gide was of the same mind, but we had decided to sit here and sit we must, because neither one of us cared to seem fastidious. Then the lady sang a song which was nothing but one of Chopin's nocturnes with ghastly words added to it, and Gide, who is a great admirer of Chopin's, moved uneasily in his chair. After this, the orchestra played a few well-known pieces and, of course, anything like a conversation was out of the question. Once in a while he would ask what they were playing, and I would answer gloomily: 'It's "Anitra's Dance" from *Peer Gynt*,' or 'It's something from *Scheherazade*.' Thus the night dragged on, and when we had had all that the flesh could bear, we finally left and Gide drove me home in a taxi. I calculated that we had spent five hours together and that I knew as little of him as he did of me.

My reason for mentioning this is that it shows a famous writer in an unaccustomed light. Later, what he called the crystal wall that stood between us was shattered and that friendship began which has meant so much to me in the last fifteen years. The last I heard of him was in Bordeaux, in June 1940. It was at the Préfecture de Police, in a crowd of distracted people who did not know what to do or where to go. Gide's nephew[20] was there, calm and smiling in spite of everything. I asked him if, in the face of a German occupation of France, Gide had not better try to go to America, because Gide is precisely the kind of person the Germans detest, I mean a free man. His nephew agreed. He then told me that he had sent his uncle a telegram to that effect (Gide being then in a small town in Southern France) and that the answer had come within a few hours in another telegram worded as follows: 'I shall stay on, and on, and on.'

In France as well as in other countries, I suppose, it is the ambition of every writer to be read by the younger generation, because the young generation hands on the books it likes to the following generation and thus the gap is bridged, or so our author fancies. In the eyes of the young generation, it is dreadful to be more than thirty, because as everyone well knows, the brain ceases to function after thirty. So when a writer is forty, of fifty, or older, he must make a show of boldness to prove to the young generation that his brain is still alert and to rehabilitate himself in their eyes. Now, Gide is over seventy, and yet he is probably the most widely read French writer among university students or writers still in their twenties, and the reason for that is that he has all through these years been able to retain that extraordinary youthfulness of spirit which is so appealing.

Another writer who appeals to the young for the same reason is Jean Cocteau. He is a very different type of person. One might almost describe him by saying that he is not at all like Gide. Gide is reserved and at times diffident, moderate in his statements, striving above all to be accurate in what he says, averse to any kind of show. The impression made by Cocteau is quite of another order. To begin with, he wishes to create an impression, whereas if Gide wishes to create any impression at all, it is the impression that he wants to create no impression whatsoever. Cocteau wants admiration, which is perfectly legitimate in a man so splendidly gifted. He is small, very thin, with a very white face, a straight, pointed nose, quick, sparkling black eyes, and above his forehead a sort of black bush very carefully trimmed. He dresses in an unusual way, wears flashy ties and sweaters of startling colors, unbuttons his sleeves and turns them back so as to show his shirt cuffs and leave greater freedom to his bony, intelligent hands, which he is perpetually waving about in marvelously descriptive gesticulation. Of all the writers I have ever met, he is probably the most singular in aspect, the most brilliant and entertaining in his talk, and, I have little doubt, the nearest in approach to the celebrated talkers of the eighteenth century. He comes into a room full of dull or silent people, and all of a sudden everything seems to be ablaze with wit. Laughter precedes him. Before he has even shaken hands with you, you are rocking with laughter at some funny remark he has made on entering the room and all of a sudden you feel that you too have funny remarks to make, because there is something very contagious about Cocteau's form of wit; it seems to do something to your brain, it wakes it up, it sends electricity through it, and you realize with a shock of pleasure that the world you are living in is not the humdrum place you imagined, but a very exciting world perpetually full of new thoughts, new sensations and new mysteries. In just a few words Cocteau can sum up and clarify a mass of confused thinking which has been your own thinking for years, and he does it in such an irresistibly amusing way that you can no more control your laughter than you can keep yourself from breathing. However, once he has left and you try to remember what he said, you may catch yourself wondering, wondering what he said, and how he said it. You try to write it down, but somehow you can't do it very well: the sentences seem slow and a little heavy, and when you reread them, they seem dead. They have lost almost everything: their flashlike rapidity, their spark, their life. The magician is no longer there to animate and you feel depressed and a little stupid when you look at these bits of coal which a few minutes before were diamonds.

I have mentioned his unconventional appearance. It is quite in accord with French tradition, with Gautier's bright red waistcoat and Baudelaire's eccentricities.

But Cocteau would never have dyed his hair green like Baudelaire, he is too subtle for that and also there lurks in him,

way back in the secret recesses of his soul, something of the
bourgeois spirit which prevents him from doing certain things.
In the words of Gide, he knows exactly how far it is wise to go
too far. He goes too far within certain limits. Nevertheless he is
a strange-looking person and he wants to be strange-looking. I
remember that one day, two or three years ago, my sister and I
had invited him to lunch and he arrived a few minutes late in a
state of indignant agitation. We were in the hall and he was so
perturbed that he forgot to shake hands with us. 'Anne,' he
asked, 'do I look like a tramp? Now tell me: do I look like a
tramp?' Well, he didn't look like a tramp, but he wore a very
small pointed hat on top of the black fuzzy bush I have
described, and an extraordinary little overcoat which came no
lower than his sleeves and was lined with flaming red flannel.
He then explained that our concierge, who was more like a wild
beast than a human being, had refused to let him come up the
front stairs and insisted on his taking the back stairs. She
thought, I suppose, that her front stairs would be dishonored
by the clownish hat and that red flannel. A violent argument
had taken place at that point, and I regret having missed it as it
must have been picturesque to the extreme.

At heart, Cocteau will always be a schoolboy. Sometimes
there is something in him that tells him that it is time he grew
up and stopped playing pranks, and he tries to be serious, but
he is not then at his best. He should have lived at a time when
people were more lighthearted than circumstances allow them
to be at present. Around 1925 Cocteau's gaiety was one of the
very best things Paris had to offer, but I have sometimes had
fears that tragedy could do nothing else to him than thwart that
delightful spirit of youth which endears him to so many. And
yet there has been around him an atmosphere of tragedy; nor
does he seem absolutely averse to it, because he thinks of
himself primarily as a poet, and tragedy becomes a poet. The
events of June 1940 and the following months have been one of
the greatest trials Frenchmen have been subjected to, and

tragedy has become a part of their daily lives. Laughter under such circumstances is a form of courage, and I feel sure that it is not lacking, even now, in the land of Molière.

Writers I Have Known

Written for a lecture at Mills College, a women's college in California, on August 3, 1944. The same lecture was subsequently given at various other California colleges.

One of the most curious effects of great events like the present war is to alter our conception of time and to somewhat modify what might be called the perspective of memory. To say that five years stand between us and the first days of the war is only partly true. There are moments when it does not seem true at all, when we feel that a whole lifetime has gone by, and we are inclined to believe the philosophers who say that time does not exist.

It is a little alarming to begin by expressing doubts as to the reality of time. What I mean to say is that as far as the impression made upon us by time is concerned, we are separated from 1939 by a far wider gulf than, let us say, 1934 from 1929. In 1934, 1929 still seemed within our reach. We could touch it; it was familiar; it was really a part of ourselves. Not so 1939 and the years immediately preceding the war. That period belongs to another age. We look back on those remote days with mixed feelings of sadness and longing, because we fear that many things that were great and good have disappeared forever.

I, as a writer, sometimes wonder if we shall ever see again the same kind of literary activity as that which obtained in Paris between, roughly, 1920 and 1940. It is yet too soon to decide whether that period was a great one or not, from a literary standpoint. It was certainly a very fruitful one. There were enormous facilities for anyone who chose, I do not say to be a writer, but at any rate to come out in print. The French have always been great readers. Moreover, they like to own books. They don't borrow the latest novel from a public library, they buy it and keep it, and they buy it (did in those days) because books are relatively cheap in France. For those reasons a moderately well advertised author could expect to live, not uncomfortably, by his pen in the golden years of 1925, '26, '27, '28 and even '29. The struggling young author who lived in a garret and missed two meals a day was an extinct specimen

and seemed as remote as the dodo bird. Your budding genius of
1925 often went from the Ritz bar to the most fashionable
literary salon in a car which might well be his own, if he knew
how to be firm with his plublishers and wrote like Morand. He
actually lived on his royalties (was ever a grander name given
to money?). But those who couldn't, or wouldn't, write like
Morand and simply wrote like themselves, even those managed
somehow, and took the streetcar. Happy days.

There were several well-known literary drawing rooms.
(How strange that past tense applied to a world which still
seems so very close.) Some literary drawing rooms were very
serious with a faint but unmistakable suggestion of dullness.
Those were modeled on the old-fashioned nineteenth-century
reunions where philosophical conversations reigned supreme,
the fate of man was solemnly discussed and tremendous whacks
were taken at the universe. It is commonly said in Europe that
the nineteenth century ended in 1914, but it was still in its death
throes around 1925. I once found myself in Mr. Doumic's[21]
drawing room and can still remember my feeling of intense
bewilderment when I looked around me and beheld a bygone
age. Names which I knew only through my school-days
anthologies materialized into faces and voices. I shall not give
you those names, because I do not want to seem flippant or
disrespectful. As a matter of fact, I felt profoundly respectful
that afternoon. A monocled gentleman[22] some of whose verse I
had committed to memory when I was younger was good
enough to ask me if I was engaged in writing a new book, and I
answered briefly that I was. Young men in Mr. Doumic's
drawing room were supposed to answer briefly, not to talk
overmuch, not to shine. They were encouraged to listen. They
were made to feel that the world did not belong exclusively to
young scamps who had fought in the last war (with emphasis
on last) and who were trying to bolshevize literature, but to
their elders and betters, to that fearful nineteenth century with
its draped doors and ponderous affirmations. So we sat in a

circle with our feet on a fine Aubusson rug, and tea was handed around with strict observance of the rules of precedence. I can't say that I was disagreeably impressed. In a vague sort of way I wondered what would happen if the name of Lenin were mentioned, or worse still, that of James Joyce. They were, I suppose, on other occasions, with the correct tone of disapproval. It was really very interesting and I asked myself if I too, in time, should have the same attitude of mind towards the future (and inwardly prayed that I wouldn't).

I well remember how close I felt to the nineteenth century on the day I met Mme Alphonse Daudet, who died almost a centenarian in 1940. I met her in 1935, certainly not before. She received me in a drawing room made somber by heavy mahogany furniture and heavy dark paintings on the walls, one of those paintings being the famous portrait of Alphonse Daudet by Eugène Carrière, who saw the world through a brown mist and, in this particular instance, made Daudet look like a drowned man in awful need of a haircut. Daudet's widow spoke to me from the other side of a tremendous gulf of time which we both perilously tried to vault. She was amiable and talkative. For a moment or two she made a gallant effort to talk about world affairs, and the dreary names of Hitler and Mussolini were mentioned, but it was not long before she withdrew into the golden age of the Third Republic and told me about the writers she had known and liked. Oh, Flaubert was such a delightful person, so gay, so generous hearted and always ready to enjoy a good joke, when, in his booming voice, he did not inveigh against the bourgeois. And Renan. She was so fond of him. I remember the words she used to describe him, they were so curious and rang so true: '*C'était un réjoui sans cause.*' Meaning that he was lighthearted and happy for no apparent reason. Taine, the great historian of the Revolution, Hippolyte Taine she did not like so much: he was too serious, almost grim, but M. Renan, ah, he always had a smile.

Since I mentioned Mme Alphonse Daudet, this may be as

good a time as any to mention the more famous of her two sons, Léon, whose political opinions I did not share, but who interested me from a purely objective point of view. It is always amusing to observe people, and Léon Daudet was a golden opportunity for a novelist, too much so, in fact: I mean that, had I taken it into my mind to put him in a book, he might have seemed unreal. He was like a character invented by a novelist; he said and did what one expected him to do, only he said and did it in a violently unexpected way. Everything about him suggested violence. His name meant riots and pitched battles with the police. To mention this name was like throwing a hand grenade; it could not go by unnoticed.

Editor of *L'Action Française* and one of the leaders of the royalist movement, he was a short, thickset person, with a small hooked nose, very full lips, fat cheeks, and angry little eyes. His normal state of mind was one of irritation. One of his favorite pastimes was to stand at the head of his followers in a public square or in the middle of the street and to hurl deadly insults at the government, or rather at the Third Republic, commonly referred to as the old hag in royalist circles. When the order to disperse was given by the commissaire de police, Daudet and his men would answer with jeers and taunts, and the fight was on. Sticks were brandished, hats flew in every direction, and the pharmacists in the neighborhood had a busy time after the fray. Although he was cordially detested by many, this agitator's doings always made good reading in the papers. On one occasion, he was clapped in jail by the authorities. The jail was the Prison de la Santé, but he was not there very long. After a few weeks, the director of the Santé received a telephone call which made him wince: 'The Minister of the Interior speaking,' said a voice. 'Release Léon Daudet immediately.' The director was a little puzzled, but orders were orders, and Léon Daudet was hustled out of jail within that hour. It was not until the royalist leader had left Paris and crossed the Belgian border that his paper gleefully revealed that a hoax had been played on the government: one of the *Action Française* men, who had a talent for imitating people's voices, had impersonated the Minister of the Interior and given the order of release and, of course, Paris shouted with laughter.

However, apart from being a sort of political *enfant terrible*, Daudet was also a very able writer, but he wrote too much. Almost every morning, an article of his came out in the *Action Française*. These articles, as a rule, dealt with some aspect of the political problems of the day, but they were sometimes purely literary in character. Daudet had a trick of writing about Rabelais, or Diderot, or English poets or the correct way of preparing a really delicious bouillabaisse when the political situation was particularly tense and everybody expected an article on the coming war, which, by the way, he foresaw as early as 1919, or on the Revolution, which never came, but which he predicted at frequent intervals with the obstinacy of a prophet. He could be very brilliant when he wrote about the French Renaissance, particularly about Rabelais, whose truculent style he tried to imitate. He also wrote a very clever and colorful book about Shakespeare and several priceless volumes on the literary circles of Paris in his time. They are indispensable to anyone who wishes to form a complete idea of what literary Paris was like between 1890 and 1920. Daudet was anything but impartial as a memorialist. When he liked anyone, he was incurably blind to his defects. On the other hand, his wits were sharpened and his talent heightened by antipathy. He gives us an unforgettable portrait of Émile Faguet, for instance, whom he loathed. Faguet for many years was considered a sort of oracle of French literature. He was so completely obsessed by the idea of seventeenth-century perfection in the matter of style that he wrote and spoke in what he considered the manner of Vaugelas[23]. I can never think of this dreary person without recalling Daudet's description of him as Faguet stood, one very wet day, drying himself in front of the fire, his back turned to the hearth, his coat-tails trussed in the approved fashion, and smelling, says Daudet, like an old turkey being roasted with all its feathers. I did not concur with Daudet's political views, and knew him only slightly, but we had lunch together one day, in that old-fashioned dining room of the rue de Bellechasse with the shadows of Alphonse Daudet, and Taine, and Renan, and Flaubert floating in and out. What struck me in Daudet's appearance was his obviously great physical strength. He was nearing seventy. Yet he looked as robust as a bull, and indeed he has often been compared to a bull, but if he corresponded to anything in the animal world, it seems to me he was much more like a wild boar, with tusks ready to gore and little hoofs eager to trample on the dead enemy. He spoke and drank abundantly. Glass after glass of Burgundy and Graves was tossed down in a manner reminiscent of Brother Jean des Entommeures[24], and I could not help remembering, by contrast, the way Maurice Barrès behaved at dinner parties; when four or even five glasses of wine were placed in front of him (as they do in France), he would take up one glass after the other, hold it under his long disdainful nose for a second or two, just to breathe in the exquisite aroma, and put it down again untasted. Daudet considered that a quart of wine was what a man needed with each meal; I admired him in this. He was an excellent talker, if uninterrupted, but he lacked the mental agility of a Cocteau, he was not quick witted and totally incapable of anything like a nuance or a hint, but he had an impressive number of good stories which he told well, and he could be very funny, grossly funny, at almost any political figure's expense.

I was introduced to him by his brother Lucien, whom I knew quite well, an altogether different kind of person. Lucien Daudet was as fastidious and intellectual a person as ever walked out of Marcel Proust's books. This can be taken in a more or less literal manner. He knew Marcel Proust as well, if not better, than any man of his generation and may well have served as a model for the great writer, or at least sat, unconsciously, for one of those admirable composite portraits which we find in *Swann's Way*. He looked like his father without a beard and with close-cropped hair, but Alphonse Daudet had a benevolent expression, whereas Lucien held the world at a distance with a somewhat haughty look. He could hardly disguise his feelings of repulsion or boredom on seeing certain faces that were, to borrow a phrase from Stevenson, smoothed by hypocrisy. He mistrusted almost any kind of political activity and lived in a world of memories. An omnivorous reader, he spoke delightfully of books and characters he had known and expressed himself with extreme care; any untidiness of speech or, for that matter, of dress brought a glance of bitter, if silent, disapproval. This gaunt man who gazed at the world through a most forbidding monocle was at heart the kindest and most affectionate of beings, but this he concealed with studied coldness. He, too, like a great many literary people, had become like a character in a book instead of remaining the kind of material which a novelist uses for a book.

One seldom saw him at literary gatherings, which he considered rather debasing. He was the son of a man who had refused to besiege the Academy and beg forty Academicians to vote for him, and anything that smacked of literary strategy filled Lucien Daudet with dire contempt, but I think he was wrong in suspecting the salons of his day. Writers met there because they took pleasure in seeing each other and talking, or, as the case might be, in seeing each other and not speaking. At times there were rows and visiting cards changed hand, which meant blood, not much blood, as a rule, just a few drops trickling down the fleshy part of the arm, somewhere in the Bois de Boulogne.

There were several types of salons. Some were grand, some were modest. The grand ones were too big, the modest ones were too small, or so it seemed. Why was it that a little woman

who was neither very pretty nor very well read could pack her
small drawing room with celebrities, whereas Le Comte de So-
and-So's magnificent parlors, with their Bouchers and their
Fragonards, and their liveried servants opening and shutting
doors, remained all but empty, save for four or five musty
remnants of the preceding century? Because the little woman
had wit and charm and made everyone laugh, while Le Comte
de So-and-So, who owned one of the most respectable maga-
zines in France and several châteaux in Touraine, had nevertheless one foot firmly planted in his grave and the other
already raised to follow.

The modest salon I have in mind was located not very far
from the Place de l'Étoile[25]. Two small rooms in a small house,
two small rooms overcrowded with Directoire and Louis-
Philippe furniture. At five o'clock, on certain days, it was empty
and very quiet. Just a pug snoring on the sofa and a short,
rather frail-looking woman seeing that the flowers were right
and that there were enough ashtrays; and then, fifteen minutes
later, the place was full of men and women talking and laughing
and saying such amusing things that it seemed a thousand
pities all could not be taken down in shorthand, words so
excellently put together that struck the air (rather thick by
now) and were immediately forgotten. What remains of a
conversation in which Mauriac and Giraudoux each struggled
to be heard above the hum of voices? Nothing, as far as I know.
Only a few chance remarks which some of us may have
recorded in our diaries. I am not going to harp on that subject
again, but I must say that I have always been appalled at the
thought of all the good talk that is lost in Paris, or other centers
of culture. To think, for instance, that Marcel Proust spoke
literally for hours at a time explaining what he thought of the
world he lived in, describing its subtle and ever-changing
beauty to men and women who could not always see it,
although they were a part of it. And they left him, carrying
some of his marvelous, meandering sentences in some corner of

their memories, and thought what a strange and fascinating person he was, that Marcel, but oh, how complicated, how frightfully and abnormally intelligent! A day or two passed; other things filled their minds, then they would remember that Marcel had said this or that, and diligently misquoted him to friends, and thought: 'What a clever person I am to have remembered Marcel's remark about a distant storm cooing like a turtledove or a creaking door making a sound like the opening bars of *Lohengrin*, or was it *Parsifal?*' Some of those remarks they later found in his books, but many were lost forever, whereas the heavy and utterly futile speeches of senators are recorded for all time in the state archives, where, it is to be hoped, busy little teeth will finally get the better of them.

When I met François Mauriac in 1924, I had read a few of his novels which irritated me almost as much as I admired them. I disliked the author's view of humanity but I loved the way in which he expressed all the bitterness that was in him. He used the French language much as a very talented violinist uses a Stradivarius, only I didn't care for the tunes he played, for the waltzes he mixed up with variations on the *Dies Irae*. And then his characters. They said such unkind things, and so brilliantly too, at times; they were malevolent in such a subtle way, they laughed and you laughed with them, louder and louder until you realized they were laughing at you, and at themselves. There was poison in their words and poison, not metaphorical poison, the real stuff, in neatly folded envelopes which they might or might not be carrying in their pockets. They sneaked in and out of sick people's rooms just as they sneaked in and out of churches. They seldom washed, they were not agreeable to look at, and then, all of a sudden, they did or said something which touched you almost to the verge of tears — they were human alter all.

When I first saw Mauriac, I realized that there was a subtle family likeness between the characters in his novels and their spiritual begetter. Let me, however, hasten to point out the

differences, lest I be accused of libeling a writer I admire and a
friend of long standing. Mauriac did not carry arsenic or
strychnine in his waistcoat pocket: what one would probably
have found there was a rosary. Also, whatever venom his
tongue distilled immediately found its antidote in a look or a
smile which drew a shout of laughter from the victim. Mauriac,
like a great many Parisians, has a rather ferocious form of wit.
His remarks are deadly; but this must be said of them, that they
are never so cruel as when they are directed against himself. He
is a ruthless critic of his own person. He is quick to see the
foibles of humanity, but his own shortcomings are the object of
his most murderous satire. This unceasing war which he wages
against himself is one of the most curious aspects of his very
peculiar talent. Many of his characters are simply the reflection
of what he most detests in himself. He is a pessimist about the
world because he is primarily a pessimist about Mauriac.
Hence the extraordinary verve and felicity with which he
describes his murderers and murderesses: they are constantly
and indefatigably murdering the author who is constantly and
indefatigably resuscitating in order to receive more pistol shots
and drink more poison.

Much of this can be read in his lean, almost ascetic face
which, he claims defiantly, is the ugliest in the whole of France.
This, of course, is only his way of lashing out against himself. I
could never see him without thinking how much at home he
would have seemed in the seventeenth century, wearing perhaps the dour black cloth and the prim white collar of Port-
Royal and indeed there is a Jansenist touch in his view of
present-day society. He is a Jansenist who has made his peace
with the church of Rome but not with the world, which he
considers with extreme disgust corrected by a deep feeling of
pity.

As I talk about him, I can almost hear him savagely making
fun of this or that person with that delightful Bordeaux accent
which has never left him. He is a thin, gaunt man with a sallow

complexion and the saddest eyes imaginable except when they
suddenly light up as he is about to make one of his irresistible
jests. Among the many recollections I have of him, none, I
think, is quite so vivid as that of an evening we spent together
walking through the streets of Paris and talking about people
we knew. Mauriac was in extremely good spirits and laughed
so heartily at his own jokes that he actually doubled up, with
both hands thrust in his overcoat pockets and tears coursing
down his cheeks. At other times, when religion was uppermost
in his thoughts, he could be as serious as a reformer and spoke
of the utter vanity of the world with an earnestness which filled
his listeners with what Emerson might have called 'quiet
despair.' He was at once the gayest and the most disillusioned
man I have ever known. What made him so singular was that
extraordinary gaiety of his, but we all know that no gaiety can
be quite so loud as that of a real pessimist.

There is something definitely provincial about Mauriac. His
accent, his general attitude towards people are not those of a
Parisian, but were he not provincial he would not be Mauriac
and his talent would lack much of its flavor. It was very
provincial of him never to miss the weekly reunion at the
drawing room I have mentioned. I don't think he would mind if
I said that he is an inveterate gossip, eager to hear the latest bit
of scandal about his nearest and dearest friends, but having
satisfied his curiosity, ready to take up the cudgels for them.
Anger lends him a marvelous readiness of speech and his
retorts had an unforgettable sting.

One day he had a very vehement argument with Paul
Souday, then one of the most influential critics in Paris.
Souday, who wrote for *Le Temps*, had the physique of an old
musketeer on the verge of apoplexy. He reminded one a little
of Falstaff, but a somber, disagreeable Falstaff. When he
damned a book, there was not very much to be done about it, as
Le Temps had a wide circulation. That week he had torn
Mauriac's novel[26] to shreds, and the next day he and a very

resentful Mauriac met and glared at each other in the crowded little drawing room. Mauriac opened hostilities by refusing to shake hands with Souday, and forthwith accused him in a ringing voice of not understanding the books he reviewed and of willfully misrepresenting the author's meaning. It was a grave accusation and Souday gave a sort of grunt of anger. He offered to step outside with Mauriac and settle their argument in the street. 'I shall not stand being attacked by you in the presence of twenty people' he said. 'Indeed', retorted Mauriac, 'but *you* did not hesitate to attack me in front of twenty thousand people.' And the row ended then and there in shouts of laughter.

As I look back on those days and remember how easy it was to see the most famous French writers of the period, I bitterly regret not having attended more literary gatherings of the type I have described. I was something of a stay-at-home. I loved my books and the view I had from my windows which looked out on the Champ-de-Mars. I had friends, to be sure, but I never felt the urge to seek out celebrities.

Once or twice a year, never more often, I put on my hat and gloves, crossed the Champ-de-Mars and went to one of the big literary reunions at a well-known writer's house. The parlor seemed as large as the waiting room in a good-sized station, and a busy, good-natured hum greeted the newcomer, the buzz and murmur of a hundred French voices telling anecdotes or expressing ideas in that half-subdued and slightly excitable tone which gives conversation in France something of the quality of a talk between conspirators.

Let us try to imagine that we are there, towards the end of an afternoon in May. The tall French windows have been thrown open. The horse chestnuts and plane trees are visible against the light blue sky, darkening the huge room and its handsome Chinese lacquer wardrobes on either side of the door. A mass of white peonies gleams in the middle of a long, low table. All around, the guests are standing holding a cup or a glass as a sort of defensive weapon. What can they fear? Indiscretion? Not really. André Gide told them a long time ago that there is no such thing as an indiscreet question and that there are only indiscreet answers. What they really fear is a discreet answer that might kill conversation. They provoke conversation and if it is good, they will see to it that it does not die too soon; their half-raised glass or china cup is an invitation to talk on. Let anything be said, if it be well said, if it bring a smile to the eyes of the listener and quicken the pace of his thoughts.

Of course, it is difficult to say very much. A crowded drawing room is not the place for a leisurely talk with one person. There are too many people one wants to see, if only for a minute or two. This portly gentleman with broad shoulders is Paul Claudel. It does not seem possible to pass him by. There he stands as massive as a boulder and almost as unemotional. One cannot imagine him stooping or bending over, or waving an arm, or running, or, oh no, dancing, but there he stands in a monumental sort of way, and he stands in this drawing room as he stands in modern literature, head and shoulders above many, as grave and meaningful as one of those prehistoric monoliths which one sees on the solitary moors of Brittany. For even in the midst of a crowd he seems alone, surely one of the marks of greatness. His heavy, stern features might put an American in mind of the Great Stone Face[27]. He says little and what he says is uttered in a deliberate and somewhat peremptory tone of voice. His smile is a tigerlike grin. He is not at ease in these reunions, he is not happy. He came because he had to, but there is too much noise, too much unnecessary noise; too many vain words are bandied for which those who have uttered them will be made to account some day, and one can well imagine. M. l'Ambassadeur leaving this drawing room and saying 'ouf'.

There is another poet with us today, but how very different. A thin little man with iron-gray hair and pensive blue eyes: Paul Valéry. His reputation as a great intellectual poet might intimidate a rather bashfull beginner, but the bashful beginner would quickly be reassured by the poet's manner. No face could be more human or kinder than Valéry's, a lean, sensitive face with a half-amused smile whenever the conversation threatens to take too serious a turn, for Valéry is a real Mediterranean, not only a Latin at heart but something of an Athenian. He dreads anything ponderous. He is of the opinion that the gravest questions can be agitated provided a little wit is introduced, and he is always ready to oblige with some of his own. Like all well-known writers, he has what might be called his legend, and his monocle is a part of that legend. It is rarely in his left or right eye for more of a second or two. It hugely drops with a rather startling suddenness and is caught by a long black ribbon. Its principal use is apparently to provide Valéry with something to play with when he is talking. It flies about in circles which grow smaller and smaller as the black ribbon rolls around the poet's finger. Then the ribbon unrolls and the monocle revolves in circles of increasing radius. Obviously, it is not meant to impress as was Robert de Montesquiou's or Bony de Castellane's or Edmond Rostand's — that sham great poet — or to terrify bores as was Whistler's monocle. It is a goodnatured monocle that is never taken seriously by his owner. Maybe it helps him to think as a walking stick helps a novelist to concoct a story.

In spite of his growing fame, there is nothing solemn about Paul Valéry. He does not hope to be understood by more than a few, he is embarrassed by compliments of the variety known as flowery, above all he sincerely resents being called *maître*. If anyone wishes to talk, Valéry is always eager to hold his peace and, sometimes, to listen. As it happens, that day someone does wish to talk. A voice is heard at the far end of the parlor and as it draws nearer the great murmur of conversations subsides until the clear, shrill tones reverberate in a now completely silent room. Everyone knows whose voice it is, of course. It couldn't be Colette's. Colette has a rich, deep voice, with a Burgundy accent, and then Colette would not talk that way, wouldn't say the things that voice is saying. It could not be Simone's voice. Simone's voice is just as loud and pitched just as high, but it lacks the authority which this one possesses, and we may as well try to slip out while an opportunity offers, if we don't care for the voice in question, because it belongs to Anna de Noailles, and it is not going to stop until its owner leaves the room.

The small, delicate woman comes in slowly, walking as if she knew less about walking than about flying, and indeed there is something about her which suggests a bird, a wounded bird. Cocteau says that she has the face of a swallow, a very broad face with such very large eyes that they make it difficult to notice the other features, the tiny mouth from which such magnificent words are coming out. They are the words of a poetess who is conscious of her genius, but however proudly they may ring, they do not entirely convince us. This woman's eyes speak a different language. The tongue may tell a tale of triumph, but there is defeat in the look that goes quickly from person to person, as if it were asking for approval.

Anna de Noailles is not quite aware of this. She does not realize that the tragic quality of her beauty is due to the fact that despair is already in her heart. She is still admired by many, but Maurice Barrès, who thought so highly of her poems, is now dead, and the present generation is suspicious of what she has to say. She is famous but she is not read, that is, she is not read by those who could help her to survive. She is watching the dark shore of the future mentioned by Baudelaire, but she knows that she will not reach it. Mauriac, who is always ready with a good phrase, says that she is being slowly killed by the empty spaces around her. Of course, the spaces around her are only metaphorically empty. People still crowd to hear her, but, nevertheless, she is alone, and when she talks, she is really intoxicating herself with words to try to forget that she is alone. Her best line, her finest gift to French literature, is also an unparelleled description of herself: '*La bouche pleine d'ombre et les yeux pleins de cris.*'

On and on does the pythoness talk, but in a little while her oracle will no longer be heard. She may talk about broken pillars in the silver light of Greece, or of the black wine that is drunk in Chio, or the sinister politics of the times, but she is no longer intelligible, she is already communing with the dead.

Not very far from the spot where she stands, an unhealthy-looking young man is observing her with an eye which has the color of steel. He whispers something to his neighbor, carefully brushes back the long wisp of auburn hair that is perpetually falling across his brow, and before you know it, he has made for the door and vanished. That was André Malraux. His books are being read by the frightened and admiring bourgeois whom he wishes to see disappear.

It has now been many years since Anna de Noailles left this world, the writers who gathered to listen to her are dispersed, and the room where she held forth is, presumably, empty and silent.

On Paris

This was written specially for an exhibition in New York of pictures of Paris in December 1943. The paintings had been lent by different New York museums. The text was published in *Commonweal*. There is also a book of essays on Paris by Julian Green, published in a bi-lingual edition (Marion Boyars 1991), with photographs taken by Green himself.

As I look at all these pictures of Paris on the walls around us, I cannot help thinking that a few years ago, let us say three years ago, I would have found it difficult to enter this room and see an exhibition of this sort. Three years ago, most of us, I am sure, could not look at a view of Notre-Dame or of the Tuileries without mixed feelings of longing and sorrow, whereas in December 1943, although the longing may still be there, sorrow has slowly given way to hope and to more than hope, to the certainty of better days. We now look at a view of the Seine or of the Boulevards with sadness because we cannot forget the sufferings of the city we love, but we can reasonably say that some day, no doubt, we too shall be walking under the trees of the Grands Boulevards, like the people in that picture, we too shall stand once more on the Pont-Royal and watch the barges floating majestically down the Seine towards Saint-Cloud.

It is a curious fact that we sometimes think of the places we love as people, with souls and bodies and features, and Paris, to many of us, is a person, a great and generous person, a bold, proud and impatient person with a kind heart and a quick temper. Anyone who happened to be in Paris on November 11, 1918, will understand what I mean. There were moments when, in the roar of the crowd, one felt the very soul of the great city rising above the people and filling the sky. Paris is far more than a huge conglomeration of houses with millions of men and women living in those houses, Paris is a spirit born over a thousand years ago on a small island in the middle of a stream, a spirit made wise by suffering and enriched by centuries of experience. The Germans have attempted to tame this spirit, but Paris is not at all the kind of spirit that can be tamed; on the other hand, it is useless to try to kill it by shooting hostages; that can only make it stronger.

In the pictures we are about to look at, we shall then recognize not only a city but a person we love. There is something about a Parisian landscape which is as indefinable as a person's expression. Many painters have endeavored to grasp that expression, but not all have succeeded, however faithful they may have been in their observation. There is such a thing as a good likeness of a Parisian square, for instance, and there is such a thing as a poor one. In a poor one, the trees may all be where they belong and the houses just right, yet something will be missing to make the picture completely satisfactory, and that something is Paris itself, the invisible presence of Paris, the spirit animating the light and the leaves and the shadow of the leaves on the sidewalk. On the other hand, take a picture like Pissarro's Boulevards or Van Gogh's View from his studio in Montmartre: they are so real that they almost give you a shock. That is what genius will do. Just a few people waiting for a bus in the shade of a tree, or three or four lamp-posts standing starkly against a bare sky, no more is needed to make a Parisian's heart beat faster, because that tree, that bus and those lamp-posts are Paris to him, and for that matter to all the world.

France is now going through an ordeal such as she never dreamed and I do not think that we, over here, will fully realize the magnitude of that ordeal before we see France again. Certainly one of the most tragic aspects of the present war is the silence of France. All of those among us who have tried to speak to France either through books or by other means are sooner or later almost overwhelmed by the fact that she does not answer, so that speaking to France becomes practically an act of faith. Voices go out to her and we trust that she can still hear, but for many months now, France has remained silent. Silence can mean anything: hope, despair, anger, resignation. Once in a while, to be sure, a man comes out of France and gives a message, or a slender book is smuggled into freedom, and we listen and read, but in spite of that it is difficult to form a clear and definite idea of what France is thinking. She who, since the Dark Ages expressed herself so magnificently and knew so well how to speak to mankind, is now gagged by the worst enemy

she has ever had to face. The world has been robbed of many
things since this war began, and among the most valuable of
those things are the books which France might have given us
and the pictures she might have painted. During the last war,
Matisse painted and Proust wrote, but I doubt that an exhausted and famished France can do much more at present
than struggle to keep alive. A very moving letter came out of
France twelve months ago. It was from Paul Valéry. One
sentence in that letter has never ceased to haunt me, because in
a very few words it seems to express so much: 'Here,' said
Valéry, 'I am too cold and too hungry to write.'

However, if France cannot express herself at present, some of
her children can speak for her, and among the greatest of her
children are a few of the painters who are here represented. If
France is silent, Manet and Renoir and Monet and Toulouse-
Lautrec and Utrillo will speak for her and tell us what a great
nation the Germans are trying to kill. Never has their message
seemed as vital and as moving as it does today, because it is a
message of love and of light in the darkness we are going
through. When you look at these pictures, you will be struck, I
think, as I was by the radiant serenity of the masters who
produced them. The Paris they show us is really the *Ville
Lumière*, as it was called as early as the time of Francis the First,
the City of Light, not only the city of intellectual light, but a city
on which the light of heaven shines with a particular grace. One
might even say that it was the exquisite quality of the light in
the skies above Paris which brought into being so many
magnificent painters.

On the very last day I spent in Paris, in the spring of 1940, I
had an experience which, as I learned later, I shared with many
other people: I suddenly saw Paris as if I had never seen it
before, and it looked so beautiful in the soft golden light that I
could only stand still and stare, wondering what had happened
to Paris or what had happened to me. I had no premonition of
evil things, I never thought for one minute that Paris could be

taken, and yet, probably, this is what Paris was trying to tell us all, in its own way.

The Paris we have around us today is not a tragic one, however. It is the Paris we all want to remember.

Passy

First published in French on April 24, 1943 in the French journal *Pour La Victoire* and subsequently republished on June 4, 1943 in *Commonweal.*

It is at about this time of year that the chestnut trees in Paris, the chestnut trees near the Trocadéro in Paris, begin to grow green again. There is one of them which spreads its branches over a subway grating, thriving there innocently in warm and poisonous exhalations. Its young leaves open, reach out, like hungry little hands. Soon, it will put forth its flowers which are like candles and, if I remember rightly, those candleshaped flowers will be red. It is a young tree. This precocious and high-spirited young Parisian likes the smell of the city. It is the first, with its foliage, its little colored candles, to cross the threshold into spring. In the days when that tree and I lived together in the same city, I called it the subway tree, I felt a special friendship for it, the friendliness which one has for trees only.

Ever since the Trocadéro — through a most curious phenomenon — flew away and left us only its wings, the aspect of the square has greatly changed. Some years earlier, it had pushed and shouldered its way toward the cemetery which thus had lost the graceful little stairway by which one reached the rue des Réservoirs; there were not many steps to the little stairway; when one stood on it and looked up, one saw a row of dark cypress trees announcing in terms of fixed convention the presence of the dead and separating from the living the shades of Marie Bashkirtseff and Édouard Manet. At the foot of the stairway, old Ben Franklin sat happily in the sunlight, watching the buses pass by — his bronze in-folios in a pile under his armchair. There was in all this scene a sort of incoherency which was attractive.

The rue Franklin is a lame old lady hobbling down a hill to the rue de Passy. As she passes the cemetery she looks out over a wing of the Trocadéro and one may imagine that she is standing there on tiptoe looking for what she has mislaid between the Pantheon and the Invalides. Then for a moment she looks down into the cellar-like depths of the gardens and

walks where the shadows stalk even at high noon; at the end of
the rue Le Tasse she glances swiftly toward the Eiffel Tower to
see if it is still there; and then, abruptly, she makes haste
between the tobacco shops and the curio shops, down to the
carrefour Delessert, where a dejected streetlight, at the
entrance to the rue de Passy, presides over the meeting of the
several streets.

Rue de Passy — my childhood — I can name by heart your
little shops, the stalls in your doorways where they sell stock-
ings, the signs with their faded gilt letters, the paintings on the
marbles of your dairy shops, the allegorical ceilings of your
patisseries — Coquelin's and Petit's and Bourbonneux's —
and the oyster man standing among his baskets, with his black
apron and his short knife, and the shoe shop where Lina, my
nurse, bought slippers with skyblue pompons, and the
stationer's with the flies warming themselves in the sun on the
covers of schoolbooks, and the austere hall of Nicolas the wine
merchant, and M. Baudichon's pharmacy — he wore so wonderful a beard — and the huge gold letters which, from the
dizzy heights of a balcony, proclaim the existence of the
'Chirurgien-Dentiste,' and the horse's head — it too was gilt —
above the entry to the riding academy, and the clockmaker's
where the proprietor, bent low over his work-bench, sits
devouring a little watch, and the spring-sky scent of the first
lilac branches — the flower girl with reddened fingers holds
and shelters them in the doorway of number 93 — and the
naked sheep, chastely girded with white aprons amid garlands
of laurel in the butcher shop — the vermillion striped curtains
solemnly billowing — and the delightful odds and ends in the
perfume shops, and the jars at the herb vendor's, and the
apprentices in the bakeries looking up out of their basement
windows at the legs of the women shopping, and the dogs
fighting in the street, and the carried baskets colliding against
each other like the prows of hostile galleys, and the laughter
and the shouting and the rumble of the buses dashing at top

speed through all this little world, and not crushing even a single toe, and the beautiful liquid braids tressed by the streamlet coursing in the gutter ...

In the sleepless moments that come between darkness and dawn, sometimes I tread this impossible path again, and if, as in the past, it occurs to me to carry some books to the book binder, to my friend Desnaux, who lives not far from the rue Raynouard, and if I hesitate, as in the past, between taking the rue de l'Annonciation and the rue Jean-Bologne, almost always I choose the latter because of its coal yard whose inhuman beauty has the terrifying fascination of some landscape on the moon. I look upon the black pyramids with their sides splashed with silver and the corded wood stacked in Babylonian terraces; I take pleasure in breathing there the immemorial fragrance of wood, anthracite and coke, and when I have left the coal yard through which I have been wandering, sleepwalking with my thoughts, it is a pleasure to find myself again in the little street which leads to the door of a simple village church. We meet the gentle ghosts of our childhood in that street; let us follow it once again.

Run, little man, with your schoolbooks in the satchel bouncing against your shoulders at every step, cry out aloud, shout, shout for no reason at all, for the pleasure of being on earth, on your way glance once more at the antiquary's where the gray cat sleeps between the yatagans, the parasols and the delicate fans, hasten past the embroidery shops where they put their eyes out working initials on the snow-white linen sheets, run along past the bearded pedicure at his window observing the long deserted sidewalk, hurry to the bronze lion sentinels at the Villa Fodor gates. But you go so fast that I cannot follow you. Have you escaped into the church where the candles tremble before the Grotto of Lourdes? Are you galloping down the rue Raynouard where, in the old days, cab horses used to run away? I shall not pursue you, little man, little ghost of 1908. There is too much sadness in our city and I cannot smile to you

as gaily as I would like, but take patience, the day will come
when the Seine shall flow once more between happy banks.

The Honor of Being French

First published in May 1942, in the magazine *Pour La Victoire* and posted on billboards throughout unoccupied France. It was also published in various journals and newspapers in the United States.

It is time that we speak of this honor lest the French people themselves forget it. For two years they have been told daily of their disgrace. And amidst the terrible confusion of spirit which exists among nations since France has been silenced, the most simple truths have been lost sight of.

One of these truths is that everyone owes something either spiritual or temporal to France. It appears hardly necessary to remind the world of such a self-evident fact but it seems that since the 17th June, 1940, the world has become forgetful.

For centuries France has been the one who has given, often without realizing it herself, without counting; she gave simply by being France. One took this or that from her and in return she offered more than one took. There was something for everyone, for the thieves as well as for the beggars and also for those who signed receipts — but France was careless of receipts.

Her very inventions were stolen by her neighbor who thought to turn them against her one day to destroy her. But France did not protect herself. She would invent something else, a prey to that mad generosity which has often brought her to the threshold of destruction.

When to house her God she built a church with an altar so high and an apse so large the sky itself with all its stars would have been at ease therein, Christianity covered its lands with similar Cathedrals.

And when, the prey to one of those great impatiences, she wanted to destroy a world it was enough that a little French officer sat down before a clavichord to give the world *The Marseillaise*, the rallying call for all angers.

Even in her errors she was the greatest. Her place has ever been just a little ahead of all the others. She makes mistakes that others would not dare to make. She goes to every extremity in her favors and in her prayers, and to every extremity in her

faults. Her gravest errors are those of excess. And her excesses
are a measure of her turbulent genius.

Now she is paying the price for having been too generous. For
centuries her enemies have been conniving to put her in the
place where she now lies. She troubled them. Her fortune was
an insult to the envious.

During the last years of the thirteenth century, a German
Emperor who, by a strange coincidence happened to have the
name of Adolph, cast his eyes toward France. It would be more
exact, perhaps, to say that he had his eyes fixed upon France as
had already generations of barbarians, ill satisfied with their
meager Germany. Adolph of Nassau, therefore, gazed at certain French provinces and, to see if they were afraid and if,
possibly, with an ultimatum he could avoid the cost of a war, he
informed Philippe le Bel that these provinces should be given to
him and particularly the province of Valenciennes. The King of
France then took a large sheet of parchment and, to the horror
of the defeatists of the day who already trembled in their desire
for capitulation and collaboration, he wrote in big letters these
two words, '*Trop Allemand*,' which might be translated as, 'How
German.' That was France's reply to Germany regarding this
episode. That will always be the reply of the real France to the
eternal covetousness of Germany. History tells us that the
Adolph of that time decided it was wiser to remain at home.

Today we see France so humiliated that one is permitted to
ask if this humiliation is not in scale with her greatness.
Perhaps, indeed, greatness pays by these catastrophies; perhaps she draws them to her and wears them as a crown.

We who live in the relative, how can we know the laws of the
absolute? It may be that the misfortune of France is a sign of her
election. And those who speak in such unrestrained language of
France's punishment are talking, without knowing it, of a
mystery which may one day cover them in a great confusion.
Christians well know that suffering is a mark of love. And if
France is now in calvary I cannot see that her glory is

diminished. She is there, under the heel of Germany, and it is obvious that she has found her Judas. But woe to them who dishonor her. Let nations who do not wish to suffer in their souls salute her, for the spiritual treasures of this world are, for the most part, in the hands of her whom God has much loved. She, who today is learning that her real glory was not of the flesh, will tomorrow again show us the way. For we will not always see the triumph of mediocrity in arms.

'Watchman, what of the night?' For ages anxious people have asked this question, and the night goes on — but who knows if the dawn's approach is not heralded first by a redoubling of the clouds and that perhaps, darkness must be complete before Dawn touches the mountain peaks?

The Apprentice Psychiatrist

Written in May 1920 while Julian Green was a nineteen year-old student at the University of Virginia, this short story was published in *The University of Virginia Magazine*, the author's very first publication. It was republished several times by the *Virginia Quarterly Review*.

A few people, who have known Casimir Jovite at the time this story begins, agree that he was serious-minded and studious, with a somewhat melancholy nature and very fine, eager, inquisitive eyes that looked at everything with a sort of impassioned interest. He had been for two years one of Dr. Richard's most attentive students at the École de Médecine and had shown the greatest abilities as a dissector, but his real vocation, he used to say, was the study of our nervous system, to which he soon devoted most of his time. No doubt his friends remember the juvenile enthusiasm with which he expressed himself on the subject, in a semi-scientific review of the day: 'Neurology,' he wrote, 'is where psychology and natural science merge into one. True, we can find no such thing as the soul under our scalpel, but the mind, the tremendous mind of man, we can, so to speak, trace its origins and watch its awakening and development in three pounds of greyish flesh and a net of little white threads, we can seize thought between our instruments and explore the abstract with tweezers and microscopes.' His faith in Broca was pure and immense[28].

One day — his doctor's degree was then still in the realm of possible things — he received a letter which caused him to frown, then to pace his room, then to bluster out his indignation to the walls and the yellow skull that grinned on his desk. So he would have to give up his studies because his miserly peasant of a father refused to send him any more money and wanted him to live on the farm and stop pretending to be a gentleman. How absurd! Why, he would get some money somehow and not even try to make his family understand what a splendid future lay before him. Let the poor people live among their pigs and cows, and toil the year round for the sake of saving a handful of silver pennies; there was something stronger and higher in him that bound him to the city of learning. Tomorrow, no, today, this very morning, he would start looking for a position, a reasonable position which might allow him time enough to attend lectures and study; he would hound his friends into helping him find it and free himself, at last, from the yoke of dependence on a grudging father.

So it happened quite naturally that when old Annibal-Marie de Fronsac died, stipulating that his son should be placed under the guidance of a firm hand and an enlightened mind, Casimir Jovite boldly introduced himself to the heirs, a doting old gentleman with an agreeable smile, the supposed guardian of the orphan boy, and a stern old demoiselle with cork screw curls and three rows of lace ruffles on her black satin dress. His French that morning was beautifully careful and polished, and as he was vaguely handsome and neatly dressed and moreover able to produce a kindly note from a well-known professor, the old lady accepted his offer and the gentleman nodded in approval.

Casimir bowed.

'When may I come?'

'Oh soon — very soon. M. de Fronsac wishes to go to Baden for his health and I am to accompany him, but I do not want to leave my nephew alone here and you must try to come this week.'

Casimir hurried home and packed his trunks. He would make for Passy this same afternoon, and then the days of prosperity and peace! A comfortable room in an old-fashioned house, most of the day to himself, and three, perhaps four hours with a young boy whom he would have to instruct. Of the latter he knew nothing, save that he was seventeen and of a delicate constitution, but as he rolled away from the rue Auguste Comte in a moaning old cab he said to himself hopefully that Fate, as a rule, is consistent, all good or all bad, and that the boy was perhaps quite passable, quiet and too lazy to argue about anything. He comforted himself with this thought as far as the rue de Bac where the sight of a crowd of students coming out of a fashionable school filled him with despair. He watched them a second pouring out of the doors like a throng of apes, of insolent apes with fixed narrow ideas lurking behind the obstinate or weakly brows. But the cab whisked around the corner and the vision was gone. Now the bridge was thundering under the heavy wheels and the Cours-la-Reine was in sight. There was a pleasant breeze, the Seine rippled, the plane trees waved their long branches solemnly, and hope crept back into Casimir's heart.

After supper, that evening, he sat up with his pupil for a while and then retired to his new room. He tramped up-stairs with a feeling of relief.

'Truly, an ideal pupil my fate presents me with,' he thought, 'as entertaining as a grave!'

He paused a second, with his hand on the door-knob.

'Now, if the room is as good as the rest, then I am dreaming.'

The room was small but neatly furnished.

There came a dusky light filtering through the cotton curtains, gleaming in big, silvery patches on the well polished floor. It seemed to greet the stranger as he stood at the door, it shone cheerfully on the massive low-boy and its many brass handles, on the lazy bergeres and the big heavy bed filling one third of the room with its old-fashioned baldachin and solemn green draperies.

Casimir lit the lamp and closed the window, not, however, without having looked into the narrow street winding its way between gloomy houses and ivy crested walls. The light of a distant lantern was flickering in the dusk; everything was peaceful and silent as a Flemish *béguinage*.

'Yes, I am dreaming.'

He sat down and opened a book. It was Grasset's *Human Biology*. But very soon the lines ran together and the words made no sense. The young man's thoughts were slack and his attention fugacious, and a dim, strange vision kept hovering before him like a ghost, the blurred outline of a neatly cut face with two dreamy, tragic eyes, the very eyes that had looked at him at supper, so fixed and uncanny that a feeling of uneasiness

had come over him several times. They seemed to look clean
through him, beyond him, beyond the world of matter, down
into abysses of thought and phantasy, they stared, wide open,
as if some extraordinary dream was fascinating them, dark and
sad and rimmed with faint circles of pearly blue.

'I wonder if he sees me at all,' thought Casimir. 'He looks
consumptive. That is what Mlle de Fronsac meant when she
mysteriously whispered something about an incurable affection. But she also said her brother suffered from the same evil,
and surely her brother is not consumptive.'

He remembered M. de Fronsac's apoplectic face and smiled.
Yet he could still hear the old lady whisper as she slipped on her
mittens: 'You see, he is not at all well, and Baden is the only
place that suits him. We go there twice a year.'

Night was coming and Casimir half-dozed in the voltaire
chair. A gentle rain was pattering outside, like a child's hand
drumming the window-panes. Far away there was a low
rumble of carriages and a hum of distant voices. Suddenly, the
young man was aware of very soft and beautiful sounds coming
from a remote part of the house; half rising in his chair he
listened and recognized the first notes of an old saraband
played on a rather dull harpsichord. The touch was light and
the thin music barely reached Casimir's ear, but the quiet and
solemn rhythm seized him like a powerful charm and held his
attention till the final, diminuendo bow.

And he went to sleep that night, thinking of the spell of old-
fashioned houses and worn-out harpsichords.

Next day was warm and pleasant and they sat for awhile in
the arbor. He observed the boy carefully and tried to make him
talk and reveal itself. But this was in vain. Pierre-Marie was as
stubborn as a Breton peasant. His deep black eyes looked at
Casimir with such an expression of defiance and surprise when
he was asked a question which he did not want to answer, that
the bewildered pedagogue stopped short in his sentence and
talked of other things. Pierre-Marie, then, listened atten-

tively with his face turned full towards Casimir and his eyes like
a veil over his soul. His hands twitched; he seemed incapable of
keeping them still and was continually rubbing his thumbs on
his nails in a quick, restless movement which caught the
preceptor's ready eye. They were long, intelligent, nervous
hands with pointed finger-tips and a net of heavy, purple veins
that made them look fifty years too old. 'There is the sign of
degenerescence,' thought Casimir, as he watched the withered,
palsied fingers and the emaciated wrists that seemed trans-
lucent in the sun.

He shook his head unconsciously.

'The father's, the grandfather's, the great grandfather's sins.
A heavy debt.' Pierre-Marie looked at him curiously. Casimir
felt the weight of the stare on his whole frame, coughed and
drew lines on the gravel with his stick.

He was uncomfortable and felt angry with himself for being
so. Was he afraid of a seventeen-year-old boy? He threw back
his head and resumed the conversation in a jocular tone,
looking straight at Pierre-Marie as if he wished to stare him out.

'Did you know I could see a palace from my window?'

The boy started. His hands lay open and still.

'A palace?' he echoed in a dull, unmodulated voice which
reminded Casimir of the harpsichord.

'A palace in the midst of a beautiful park and an army of
linden trees.'

Pierre-Marie moved a little.

'That palace belonged to Madame de Lamballe[29],' he
explained.

'And now?'

'Now? Well — I don't know — it is a strange house and
father did not care for me to mention it.'

'My compliments!' said Casimir to himself. 'You are successful in your choice of topics.'

However, he made one more attempt and ventured a few cautious and insipid sentences.

Once in a while Pierre-Marie would interrupt him with some abruptness and beg him to repeat some word he had not quite understood; this he did with such a pleading tone that the oddity of it could not fail to strike the young preceptor.

A few minutes since, however, a strange idea had occurred to Casimir. He gazed on his pupil's countenance with increasing interest. He remembered certain lectures of Dr. Richard, certain passages of books read a long time before. They flashed across his mind in a new light. It seemed to him as if he understood many things much better, as if the knowledge he had acquired through years of study was now beginning to throb with life and slowly awaken. But the sky blackened and the air grew fresh, as they both left the arbor and went in.

Days passed. Drowsy June had come and Casimir still hesitated. How often he had buried his head in his hands and muttered to himself, 'Well, let us decide,' in a very firm voice, and finally decided nothing.

As if he could decide —

He was tempted both ways equally and lacked willpower; he was a man of books and habits and peaceful studies, the thought of action terrified him. Out of his library, out of the world of meditation he thrived in, he was as helpless as a child and just as brave. Society interested him as would a patient with curious affections and he studied it as such with care and perseverance. But as to taking an active part in the fate of society, the mere idea paralyzed him. How had he been able to secure his present position? Probably through a lashing of his energy by brute need.

And now here was a new problem to face, a real problem burdened with entanglements and responsibilities.

Pierre-Marie was not at all well; everyone knew that, even the old family doctor who came once a fortnight and recommended tisane as a cure for every possible ailment, even that venerable idiot realized it — though dimly. And who could not read it in those eyes in which there seemed to lurk an unutterable terror of everything? How much they now betrayed of the disquieted mind in the tragic silence of the lips! How altered, too, his complexion, his manners and speech! A livid hue had crept over his cheeks and darkened the rings around the sockets. He had grown irritable and contradiction made him moan with impatience, with torturing physical pain; above all, he suffered no arguing and settled a discussion with a violent thump on the table or a blunt and slashing remark on his opponent's inability to 'handle ideas,' as he said. Often he would burst into short and somewhat disconnected sentences, questioning his tutor on peculiar subjects with a startling eagerness to obtain an answer — no, not to obtain an answer, but to hear a voice answering him. Once, at dinner, he suddenly asked what would become of the soul of a madman that would spit on the crucifix and curse the Saints; he had risen from his seat and was gasping for his breath as he leaned over the table and lacerated the cloth with his nails, then sank down with a groan of relief, he, a zealot of the Roman faith, upon receiving the answer that there was no Hell, no Purgatory, no Paradise. Then his mania for hearing 'the last word' — 'Pray, what was that word you said just now? Yes, just now, the last one.'

Of course there was but one thing to do, and that was to call a specialist from the Salpêtrière. Casimir knew that so well! But a little thin voice there was, that softly whispered in his heart: 'A specialist? Casimir — What a pity! Think of the memorandum.' For Casimir was writing a memorandum, a small, stout book, bound in black oil-cloth, in which, daily, he copied sheets of carefully taken notes. Notes on his pupil — twitching of hands, strange queries, fits of anger, depression and weeping, manias and vellications, everything; he had observed and analyzed everything with the diligence of a Benedictine friar. He had followed the slow process of the disease with a gasping interest and the horrified semi-conscientiousness of committing a crime. But curiosity was stronger in him than pity or fear, for he went on.

One day he was writing at his desk when suddenly he heard a voice shouting: 'Criminal! You have been a criminal every second of your life since the day you entered this house!'

He started and shuddered — then shrugged his shoulders and tried to write, but his hand shook and his pen spat on the orderly, print-like lines —

He stopped and thought of the Salpêtrière a moment.

After a while he went on writing.

'What will the conclusion be?' he thought one afternoon after he had copied a few pages in his book.

Quite lately he had discovered, through the servant, many things about what he called the antecedents of his pupil. These revelations which he had obtained by way of bribery (he blushed a little at the thought) had thrown a new light on his subject. It appeared that Pierre-Marie had never been sociable and cried so hard, on one occasion, when his aunt tried to take him to a party that the attempt was never again renewed. He was fond of books to a point hardly conceivable and M. de Fronsac used to say he read far too much, but Monsieur was so kind and let him do as he pleased. Then there were Pierre-Marie's solitary walks in the Bois, after supper, and then, most horrible, his ghastly experience in the park of the Hôtel de Lamballe; he had slipped in there one evening, after dark, and had nearly been choked by a madman. Since then he had never been the same.

'A letter for you, sir.'

'Thank you.'

Casimir looked at the stamp and frowned. He tore it open. It was from Mlle de Fronsac announcing the return of her brother and herself for June 15th. M. de Fronsac was much better and so delighted with the fine air of Baden that she had decided to send their nephew there next July for the summer holidays.

When Casimir read this letter he turned very pale.

Since he had realized that Pierre-Marie was deranged and had begun, with hideous amorality, to study the progress of his infirmity, he had given all his thoughts to his pupil and practically forgotten all about his aunt and uncle. Indeed he was so interested in what he now grimly called an experiment in *anima vili* that he neglected all other occupations and remained cloistered in the little house, rue Raynouard, all day long. He now bribed the servant to spy on the young man and greatly exerted his imagination to find excuses for going into his room. He tried to induce him to work in the arbor where he could very well observe him from his window, but the boy was not to be driven out of his room; he quietly locked his door, saying he had always been allowed to work where he wished and would not be bullied or wheedled into roasting in the garden. Neither would he hear of taking walks with his tutor. So Casimir had to be contented with seeing him at the regular hour for the day's lesson and sometimes at meals.

And now this letter came, ruining his hopes. What hopes? Casimir was too great a coward to dare think of them very often and very long, but he hoped for something very definite and clear.

Day by day, he had watched the evil waxing in intensity: there was no comparison between the Pierre-Marie he had met a month ago and the boy he had seen a few hours before. Now he had reached the crisis. Pierre-Marie was on the verge of insanity, his self-possession was rapidly decreasing, his faculties much weakened. There was a destructive element in his mind. Should Mlle de Fronsac return next week, as indeed she had said, she could not fail to see how deep an alteration her nephew had undergone, and that meant, of course, specialists interfering and sending Pierre-Marie to Sainte Anne or the Val-de-Grâce, to say nothing of his own responsibility being involved in the affair. Why had he not let the aunt know, or asked a doctor to examine the young man? Yet nothing was hopeless. He could still go to the Salpêtrière or Charenton, bring back a specialist and thus be freed from suspicion.

This thought he agitated awhile, not out of pity for the suffering creature entrusted to his care, but merely out of fear and selfishness. He shuddered at the thought of being arrested and incarcerated at Saint-Lazare, for the clear and pitiless voice cried within him, 'You are a criminal of the worst kind: conscious, patent and cruel!'

But stronger than this panical horror of prison life, an overpowering, longing desire to know the outcome of his experiment, to follow the development of mania from its earliest indicia to its ultimate victory, made him accept the many great risks of the adventure and, hardly thinking of what he was doing, resolve instantly on a new line of conduct.

What happened afterwards is not well known. It is probable, however, that the student's plan, such as is shown in his memorandum, received immediate execution, but any definite information is lacking. It would appear from a careful examination of the scraps of writing found in his note-book, that Casimir's scheme was first to deprive his pupil of anything that might afford peace to his troubled mind and then to aggravate and harrow him into madness.

On June 10th, a piano-tuner was sent for by Casimir for the purpose of taking apart the harpsichord on which Pierre-Marie played every afternoon, even on his worst days, and seemingly deriving much pleasure from this innocent and soothing way of entertaining his chronic ennui.

The instrument was not out of tune and Pierre-Marie, whose ear remained perfect to the last, tried in vain to dismiss the bewildered pianist; Casimir shoved him aside so brutally that the boy fell 'and lay on the floor as pale and motionless as a dead man,' the servant said, 'and with such a terrible expression that I dared not help him up.' To this Camille, the servant, whose complicity was shown upon the discovery of the memorandum, we are indebted for the little we can add to this tale.

Casimir, since he had received Mademoiselle's last letter, had acted very strangely. That he, usually so gentle with his pupil, should have knocked him down on a sudden, seemed incredible. But that was only the beginning. The same evening, he burst into Pierre-Marie's room and spoke to him in a loud, threatening voice, as one roars to a child to frighten him. Camille heard him bluster and rage for almost three-quarters of an hour, but as far as he knew, Pierre-Marie never answered him and remained absolutely silent. Then he heard the door open once more and slam violently and Casimir hurry back to his room. The tutor remained there the day after, restlessly walking up and down now muttering to himself, now sobbing, or laughing, one could not make out which. After supper (which he ate alone in his room), he went to Pierre-Marie's room and repeated the scene of the night before. It was the same thing over again.

Pierre-Marie did not move. All day long the unfortunate boy had stayed indoors. Three times the servant had gone to his room to ask him to take some food but Pierre-Marie did not even look up and apparently did not understand.

On the morning of the 13th, the preceptor told Camille he was going out to do some shopping and that nobody was to come into the house during his absence.

'See that nothing happens to Monsieur Pierre. I found him feverish and even delirious last night. But the doctor is coming today.' As he said these last words, a faint smile passed over his face, and he left immediately after.

He looked, says Camille, very pale that morning, with somewhat of a haggard, harassed expression about the eyes. He came back towards two o'clock, and without taking off his hat and gloves went up to his pupil's room.

He talked very quietly now and seemed to have recovered his gentleness of former times.

All of a sudden a pistol went off in the room, and after a few minutes of silence, someone burst out laughing, hysterically.

When the policemen entered the room, half an hour later, they found, lying on his stomach, Pierre-Marie de Fronsac, shot through the temple, and, playing in a corner with a pistol, a raving maniac.

Notes

1 Christian Sinding (1856–1941), the Norwegian composer and pianist, studied music in Munich and Berlin and wrote chamber music, lieder and piano pieces.
2 The Argonne forest, along with Clermont, Neuvilly and Vauquois, formed part of the front line at Argonne throughout the war.
3 Mr. Ware was chief of the American Field Service stationed at Argonne.
4 August 1922.
5 Henri Schmitz, a Swiss friend of Julian Green's elder sisters.
6 La Rotonde was, with la Coupole, le Dôme and le Select, one of the fashionable Montparnasse cafés frequented by painters of the time.
7 The *Echo de Paris* was an extremely conservative newspaper founded in 1884 by Victor Simond. Originally orientated towards the arts and literature, it included among its contributors Alphonse Daudet, Huysmans and Maupassant. Then it went over to the Catholic right with Barrès, Bazan and Bourget, the three Bs.
8 Jacques Maritain.
9 Green is referring here to the version by Crampon.
10 *Le Simoun* by Henri-René Lenormand, was first staged in Paris in 1922. It is set in the Algerian Sahara and, like Lenormand's other plays (*Le Mangeur de rêves*, *Le Temps est un songe*, *Les Ratés*, etc.,) the subconscious plays an important part in the action.
11 Jules Michelet, *La Mer*, 1861.
12 'Imitation is suicide', Ralph Waldo Emerson, *Essays*.
13 'The Mental Traveller' by William Blake: 'I travelled thro' a land of men . . . .'

14 'Montparnos' was the name given since the turn of the century to artists, writers and painters who inhabited the *quartier* around the boulevard Montparnasse.

15 Count Robert de Montesquiou was a very mannered poet and the basis for Proust's Baron de Charlus.

16 Reynaldo Hahn (1875–1947), the French composer, was born in Caracas. A child prodigy and student of Massenet, he finally went on to become Director of the Paris Opera in 1945.

17 Euphues was the hero of a novel by John Lyly, a character who is endowed with all superior qualities.

18 Giraudoux was a diplomat by profession. He was secretary general of the Quai d'Orsay and, on declaration of war, was appointed Minister for Propaganda by Daladier.

19 Le Traktir was the second site of the Restaurant Prunier in the avenue Victor-Hugo.

20 Marc Allégret.

21 Mr. Doumic was a literary critic and director of the *Revue des deux Mondes*.

22 Henri de Régnier.

23 Claude Favre de Vaugelas was a French grammarian and founding member of the Académie Française. His *Remarques sur la langue française utiles à ceux qui veulent bien parler et bien écrire* is still in common usage.

24 The libertine monk who appears in four of Rabelais' books.

25 The salon referred to is that of Marie-Louise Bousquet at 40, rue Boissière. Close friend of Schiaparelli, Christian Bérard and Anne Green, she was the French director of *Harper's Bazaar*.

26 *Le Désert de l'amour*.

27 'Great Stone Face' is a story by Nathaniel Hawthorne from his collection *The Snow Image*.

28 The surgeon Broca (1824–1880) specialized in the anatomy of the skull and was founder of the *Revue d'anthropologie*.

29 The palace of the Princesse de Lamballe went on to house the clinic of Dr. Blanche, where Baudelaire, Maupassant and Nerval were treated. Today it is the home of the Turkish Embassy.

Other books by Julian Green
from Marion Boyars Publishers

The Distant Lands

A novel of the antebellum South

Sixteen-year-old Elizabeth Escridge and her impoverished mother arrive in Georgia from England to seek refuge with wealthy relatives. Immersed in the South's aristocratic society — young men in morning coats duel for her favor at dawn — Elizabeth discovers a web of secrets, dark destinies and private tragedies concealed beneath the tranquil, genteel façade of Southern life. A compelling love story, *The Distant Lands* is also the story of political intrigue, of secession and above all of extravagant high society living: balls and banquets are described in minute and authentic detail.

'. . . a compelling drama of the 1850s South . . . colorful and careful historical fiction, Julian Green's opus is a delicious immersion into time and place, stylish and fluid, with an abundance of characters who attract with their humanness.'
Booklist

'The writing, the characterization and sensitivity all combine to foreshadow the doom of the elegant, aristocratic South in this epic and wonderful novel.' *The Sunday Independent*

'Green indicates that the distant lands are sublime habitations. It is a triumphant novel of pilgrimage.' *The Literary Review*

'Julian Green is . . . an astute observer of society and a subtle moralist. The prose of *The Distant Lands* is deceptively transparent, a lens, not a plane of glass.' *The Boston Globe*

'A family saga full of dark and tormented characters, it is replete with Spanish moss, gloomy mansions and family ghosts, religious fervor and guilty conscience, passionate loves that may contain a wisp of incest.' *San Francisco Chronicle*

'A tribute to the memory of his mother and to the defeated South, the lost paradise of his memories. Meticulously crafted and intensely readable.' *The Independent*

The Green Paradise

Autobiography Volume One 1900–1916

'I would like to find the gossamer thread that passes through my life from birth to death, the one that guides, binds, explains.' *Julian Green*

Autobiography, confession of adolescence, and exercise in the art of evoking past experiences ... Julian Green's memoirs of his childhood are full of many fascinations. Green's description of a happy family life reaches back to the 19th century and deep inside his burgeoning self, which he analyzes with amazing objectivity.

The main factors in the author's development are his creativity, his conversion to Catholicism and his nascent sexuality. Julian Green's determination to 'say everything' is impressive. The narcissism of youth, the anguish of his mother and the brutal realities of the human condition are all explored in the first volume of his autobiography. *The Green Paradise* closes on the young Green, aged just sixteen, joining an American contingent bound for ambulance service in the First World War.

The War at Sixteen

Autobiography Volume Two 1916–1920

After a period of training as an ambulance driver, he and his comrades were sent to the Argonne front. It was not long before the horrors of war began to make their impression on his young mind: in the summer evenings he heard the rumble of gun-fire from Verdun; his first sight of a dead soldier made him a pacifist for life.

Towards the end of 1917, the US Army took over the Field Service and discovered that Green was under eighteen. He was sent home, but undeterred, he joined the American Red Cross and found himself serving on the North Italian front.

Many years later, and by then a distinguished writer, Julian Green has recreated those early years in this moving revealing and ruthlessly honest account of his adolescence. A shy, serious and intensely devout boy who had lost his mother when he was only fourteen, his sudden and violent exposure to loneliness, suffering and death, and his first experiences of self-discovery and sexual awakening were to mark his rise to maturity and permanently influence his development as a writer.

The New York Review of Books described the French editions of

Julian Green's autobiography as 'a major achievement' and 'a singular classic of confessional literature.'

Paris

Bilingual Illustrated Edition
Translated by J.A. Underwood

Paris, Julian Green discovered very early on, when looked at on the map, takes on the shape of a human brain. This moment of recognition was an important step in the developing love affair between a man and a city. For the author, his adopted home is a street map of the human imagination. Green accompanies the reader on a stroll around this enchanted place — its secret stairways, courtyards and alleys — sharing his discoveries and sense of wonder at every turning. A stroll through a city becomes a journey through the sensitive mind of a writer and gifted craftsman. The book is illustrated with the author's own photographs of Paris.

'The tone is mainly elegiac, contrasting the charm of the old Paris of his childhood with the brashness of the new, and the style is exquisitely literary in a traditional French manner.'
New York Review of Books

'. . . the most bizarre and delicious of all this winter's travel books . . . Green does not go far from home and how sharply he reminds one that the best travel writing has little to do with length or breadth of journey, everything to do with what the travellers have with them in the bulging backpack of the mind.'
The Observer

'The pictures are truthful, unpretentious and haunting, and Green's evocation of the city poetic and unsentimental.'

Times Literary Supplement

'If you care for good writing and are interested in seeing Paris from an unusual perspective, then try this lovely and elegant book.'   *Gay Times*

'. . . full of philosophical speculations, moody reveries, flights into the past and future.'

The New York Times Book Review

South

A Play

'Can you imagine a man lacking courage to the point of not being able to speak of his love?'   *(Act Three, Scene One)*

In this drama of complex relationships and doomed love, Julian Green masterfully portrays the interaction of extremes in a significant historical setting. It is April 11, 1861, General Beauregard demands the capitulation of Ford Sumter in Charleston Harbor, and the American Civil War will begin the next day. But what does this matter to the people gathered on this torrid Sunday at the Bonaventure plantation?

The play is Green's vehicle for examining opposing elements in antebellum Southern society: the North versus the South; the white man against the black man; European values in contrast to those of youthful America; and how the sexually normal fail to understand the sexually deviant.